REPORTING
THE COUNTERCULTURE

Media and Popular Culture
A Series of Critical Books

SERIES EDITOR
David Thorburn
Director of Film and Media Studies and
Professor of Literature,
Massachusetts Institute of Technology

In recent years a new, interdisciplinary scholarship devoted to popular culture and modern communications media has appeared. This emerging intellectual field aims to move beyond inherited conceptions of "mass society" by recognizing the complexity and diversity of the so-called mass audience and its characteristic cultural experiences. The new scholarship on media and popular culture conceives communication as a complex, ritualized experience in which "meaning" or significance is constituted by an intricate, contested collaboration among institutional, ideological, and cultural forces.

Intended for students and scholars as well as the serious general reader, **Media and Popular Culture** will publish original interpretive studies devoted to various forms of contemporary culture, with emphasis on media texts, audiences, and institutions. Aiming to create a fruitful dialogue between recent strains of feminist, semiotic, and marxist cultural study and older forms of humanistic and social-scientific scholarship, the series will be open to many methods and theories and committed to a discourse that is intellectually rigorous yet accessible and lucid.

Communication as Culture
Essays on Media and Society
JAMES W. CAREY

Myths of Oz
Reading Australian Popular Culture
JOHN FISKE, BOB HODGE, and GRAEME TURNER

Teenagers and Teenpics
The Juvenilization of American Movies in the 1950s
THOMAS DOHERTY

Comic Visions
Television Comedy and American Culture
DAVID MARC

Reporting the Counterculture
RICHARD GOLDSTEIN

Forthcoming

Shakespearean Films, Shakespearean Directors
PETER DONALDSON

British Cultural Studies
An Introduction
GRAEME TURNER

Additional titles in preparation

Reporting
the Counterculture

RICHARD GOLDSTEIN

Media and Popular Culture: 5

Boston
UNWIN HYMAN
London   Sydney   Wellington

Unwin Hyman, Inc.
8 Winchester Place, Winchester, Mass. 01890, USA

Published by the Academic Division of
Unwin Hyman Ltd
15/17 Broadwick Street, London WIV 1FP, UK

Allen & Unwin (Australia) Ltd,
8 Napier Street, North Sydney, NSW 2060, Australia

Allen & Unwin (New Zealand) Ltd in association with the Port
Nicholson Press Ltd,
Compusales Building, 75 Ghuznee Street, Wellington 1, New Zealand

First published in 1989.

Library of Congress Cataloging in Publication Data

Goldstein, Richard, 1944–
   Reporting the counterculture / Richard Goldstein.
     p.   cm. — (Media and popular culture ; 5)
   Includes index.
   ISBN 0-04-445238-1. — ISBN 0-04-445239-X (pbk.)
   1. Journalism—Social aspects—United States—History—20th
century. 2. Mass media—United States—Influence—History—20th
century. 3. United States—Social conditions—1960–1980. 4. United
States—Popular culture—History—20th century. I. Title.
II. Series.
PN4888.S6G65 1988
302.23′0973—dc20   89-33757
                                                 CIP

British Library Cataloguing in Publication Data

Goldstein, Richard
   Reporting the counterculture. – (Media and
   popular culture).
   1. American popular culture, history
   I. Title II. Series
   306′.1
   ISBN 0-04-445238-1
   ISBN 0-04-445239-X Pbk

Typeset in 10 on 12 point Palatino and printed in Great Britain by
Billing & Sons, London and Worcester

For Judith G. Hibbard,
who got me through it,
and Tony Ward,
who helped me remember.

CONTENTS

Series Editor's Introduction   *page ix*

Acknowledgments   xi

Introduction: First Person, Past Tense   xiii

PART I. *The Music*   1

1. Gear   3
2. Shango Mick Arrives   9
3. Next Year in San Francisco   15
4. Harlequin in Neon   21
5. The Lizard King   33
6. More Mysterioso   41
7. Mover   47
8. San Francisco Bray   53
9. Bell-Bottom Blue Jeans   59
10. Je Fais Comme Je Veux   67
11. Ravi and the Teenie Satori   71
12. Giraffe Hunters   75

PART II. *The Mystique*   79

13. The Psychedelic Psell   81
14. Maharishi Meets the Press   85
15. A Quiet Evening at the Balloon Farm   89
16. Catcher in the Haight   95
17. The Insulated Hippie Awakens   101
18. The Long Hot Summer on Blue Jay Way   109
19. The Head Freak Awaits a New Son   113
20. A Groovy Idea While He Lasted   119

CONTENTS

PART III. *The Madness*   123

21. Theater of Cruelty: King in Chicago   125
22. Theater of the Absurd: Insurrection at
    Columbia   131
23. Theater of Fear: One on the Aisle   137
24. Homecoming   143
25. C. J. Fish on Saturday   145
26. Love and Money and the Shoot-out
    in Marin   149
27. That Good Night   161

A Note on the Text   165

Index   167

Series Editor's Introduction

The vivid, subjective vignettes of the counterculture collected here have for me a greater force than any official history. Part anthropological artifact and part spiritual autobiography, these pieces—culled mostly from Goldstein's articles and columns in *The Village Voice*—trace a passage from hopeful expectation to disillusionment that some will read as a reluctant and overdue maturing and others as a tragic or at least melancholy adjustment to historical reality.

The young author of these pieces has a keen sense of the absurd, and he understands the corrupt, extensive power exerted by those he calls (in a fine phrase from his witty essay on Antoine, the ersatz French Bob Dylan) the "merchants of novelty." He is armed not with a fully developed politics but with an aesthetic of defiance and nonconformity grounded in the culture of rock music. The limits (though also the attractions) of such an aestheticized politics are a recurring subtext or lesson in these accounts of musicians, promoters, hippies, and political protestors. Implicit in nearly every essay, this theme emerges explicitly in the final sections of Part II and in the more overtly political chapters of Part III.

"There isn't going to be any revolution," Country Joe MacDonald tells a shocked Goldstein in the troubled fall of 1968. Goldstein has come "to rap about the revolution" with the rock group that represents for him the essence of political commitment. Instead he encounters a powerful cynicism and candor. I don't know any authentic guerrillas, Country Joe remarks wearily, only "a lot of people wearing Che Guevara tee shirts . . . what a bunch of tripped-out freaks." Later in the same interview Country Joe strikes at the heart of our narrator's already vulnerable politics: "Music's nothing to believe in. I mean . . . it's just sound."

Goldstein's writing during the 1960s both reported on and participated in the distinctive forms of aesthetic experimentation that helped to define that volatile period. His book will have a double interest: as an account—an engaged, attentive portrait—of some of the characteristic figures and events of the 1960s; *and* as an artifact itself, a significant instance of the "New Journalism" to which he refers in his introduction. The more violently subjective and "fictionizing" strains of this movement—such as the work of Tom Wolfe or Hunter Thompson—are no doubt better known, but I believe Goldstein's more restrained (and less self-regarding) work has equal interest for us now. Fragmentary and intuitive, the pieces gathered here offer not a systematic but a richly evocative chronicle of a crucial moment in our recent past. They speak to us simultaneously as a commentary on that time and as an expression of it.

—David Thorburn

ACKNOWLEDGMENTS

Among the many editors who made these pieces possible, I am especially grateful to Dan Wolfe, cofounder of the *Village Voice*. He gave me my first job in journalism, and encouraged my growth without directing it. Clay Felker was an unwavering supporter, first as the editor of *New York Magazine*, and later, when he purchased the *Voice*. Sy Peck nurtured my criticism in the *New York Times*, and Mary Cantwell was a generous friend at Conde Nast.

In addition, I want to thank David Thorburn for his exacting editing of the introductory essay, and Lisa Freeman for her faith in this unusual project. David Marc and Daniel Czitrom helped me to realize that my early work could have a life beyond its origins. My parents, Jack and Mollye Goldstein, held their breath until the sixties ended: perhaps this book will convince them that risk can sometimes bring reward.

"The Lizard King" is reprinted from *New York*, where it appeared as "The Shaman as Superstar." (Copyright © 1989 by the *New York* Magazine company. All rights reserved.) "The Head Freak Awaits a New Son" and "A Quiet Evening at the Balloon Farm" first appeared in the *New York World Journal Tribune*. "Harlequin in Neon" first appeared in *Eye*. The remaining pieces are reprinted by permission of the author and courtesy of the *Village Voice*.

Introduction:
First Person, Past Tense

I had a lesson in the afterlife of artifacts recently, when I came across a torn and long neglected tie-dye. It triggered tangled memories of the sixties, when I had worn this very shirt to some auspicious interviews, dropped acid in it, went to demos, and even had sex in it. Now I wondered what to do with this sanctified shmata, much too tatty to be worn but impossible to throw away. I thought about turning it into a wall hanging, but decided instead to dispose of it the way one might part with a childhood teddy bear, by stuffing it into the recesses of a bureau drawer. But later that night, watching *Married . . . with Children*—which is to sitcoms what *Pink Flamingos* is to cinéma vérité—I noticed that Al Bundy's teenage daughter was wearing a similar tie-dye. Hers was bolder and more lurid, a slam-dancing swirl across her bosom. Whatever tie-dyes once meant to me, they'd come to signify something much more ambiguous to the producers of this kinky sitcom. I'm too tied to the original to guess what it might mean today, except to observe that, in this culture of endless recuperation, those who do not understand history are forced to wear it.

And so we see the return of the peace sign as an emblem of the embattled liberal arts major, and the paisley vest worn under a business suit to suggest that even yuppies can harbor an expressive interior. This couture is part of what is known, in the lexicon of tabloid and tube, as the sixties revival. The phrase does not refer to renewal or restoration, but to a recycling of the recent past as raw material for a brand new mythology. In this remake, the sixties are imagined as an arcadian interlude between rigidity and chaos—what the poet Geoffrey O'Brien calls "dream time." To revisit this Magic Kingdom we need only wish upon an artifact, and there is much to choose from:

the Smothers Brothers are back; the Monkees are back; there's even a new psychedelic drug, Ecstasy, to be dropped while dancing to the crypto-disco known as Acid House. Meanwhile, in the cineplex, JFK has become the patron saint of romantic comedies and earnest dramas set in that "one brief shining moment" when it was possible to conflate sex, struggle, and stereo. Of course, this image of the dream time is aimed at middle-class white Americans; for blacks, the sixties is presented as an era of purposeful solidarity, and for blue-collar whites, it is summoned up as a cautionary tale of social chaos, in which the only heroes are tormented soldiers, rogue cops, and reverent astronauts.

This is the central contradiction of the sixties revival: it is happening within a political culture overtly hostile to the sixties. Our politics are antithetical to its agenda; our response to sex and drugs (if not rock 'n' roll) is as punitive as the sixties was permissive; our dissent is as defensive as the sixties was expansive. We are, in every sense, a culture drawing in the wagons on itself—and somewhere out there, we're told, lies the very chaos engendered by the dream time, threatening to overwhelm our fragile enterprise. Yet the artifacts of that forbidden era continue to resonate with a mysterious energy: naive, yet daring; primitive, yet futuristic; exotic, yet achingly familiar. Sixties style has a tantalizing expressiveness next to the depersonalized contours of mass culture now. But what we notice most is its cogency. Within the sanctioned parameters of sensibility, the most radical aspirations achieved a form and function they were denied in politics. In art and style, the sixties worked. The remarkable consistency that runs through sixties culture contradicts our image of that decade. How could such a chaotic time have produced such coherent art? One possibility is that, though the chaos was real (and eventually overwhelming), the culture harbored a hidden logic—to use a sixties word, a vision.

Given the menace and allure the sixties still hold for us, it is no wonder the sixties revival is being staged like the masque in *Marat/Sade*. In that formative piece of sixties theater, the inmates of an asylum are trotted out before an audience of newly resurgent aristocrats to act out the excesses of the recent revolutionary past. The audience is horrified but riven by the

show, and protected by bars and armed guards. A leeri
Jacobin delivers his apologia to the "thirtysomething" (

> Please remember that we show
> Only those things that happened long ago
> Things were very different then
> Today, we're all God-fearing men.

Most movies and plays with a sixties motif carry similar dis-
claimers or create a comparable feeling of insulation by setting
the action in a rockadian haze, with elaborate scores of Golden
Oldies and state-of-the-art retro wear. These acoutremental
obsessions are not surprising, given the market for pieces
about the dream time: like the "audience" in *Marat/Sade*,
they are upwardly mobile professionals on the verge of middle age, similarly cosmopolitan and conflicted. Finally, these
retro-spectacles are being enacted in the midst of a conservative
hegemony. Are we doomed to recuperate the past as an emblem
of our helplessness to control the present, or can we get beyond
the masque?

Journalism—the art of the eyewitness—is a good place to
begin the project of freeing up the sixties from its uses now.
The counterculture of that era spawned its own brand of
journalism, a counter-reportage infused with the jargon and hy-
perbole of what was called the Hip Community. The form these
dispatches often took falls somewhere between essay and
narrative, between criticism and memoir: a hybrid generated
by a particular moment in social history, when systems and
structures—in art, politics, and (more tentatively) class and
caste—seemed frangible. Counter-reportage became the voice
of mobility on the margins. As it percolated up from hip
weeklies like the *Village Voice* to adventurous monthlies like
Esquire and *Harper's*, this rogue reporting served as a carrier
of messages between the counterculture and the mass. It remains a rich text of the sixties; yet the sixties revival has all
but passed that decade's journalism by. Its form is deemed too
capricious and its content too arcane to be of interest now. A
more likely explanation is that, at its jagged, extravagant best,
counter-reportage doesn't resemble any current literary genre.
When the moment passed, so did the style.

Looking back at these dispatches a generation later, it's clear that their underlying subject is the struggle for subjectivity. That was much trickier than it might seem. In the sixties, it was easier to devise a style than an expressive voice, easier to invent an idiom than to describe what one actually saw, easier to sparkle and sass than to expose what lay beneath—in my case, doubt. And commerce had a way of obscuring the difference between thinking and schtick. This process of injecting a commercial or institutional bias was known as "hype," and journalism was its prime target. Powerful and increasingly centralized media were beginning to blur the distinction between real and promoted events. Even TV news footage, as we discovered, could be spliced and slanted to push a product or a point of view. The first line of defense against this tainted corporate neutrality was an infusion of the personal. Subjectivity meant imposing a narrator on the news, a voice that could openly address the meaning of events. This narrator was to be, in every sense, implicated: like Susan Sontag's artist-explorer, she stood "on the frontiers of consciousness"; like Whitman, he could proclaim, "I am the man. I suffered. I was there."

Am I talking about the New Journalism here? Yes and no. Tom Wolfe, who has written a long explanatory essay on the genre, disdains the first person as a device that merely solves a lot of "technical problems. . . . In fact," Wolfe writes, "most of the best work in the form has been done in third-person narration with the writer keeping himself absolutely invisible." As for persona—the self constructed in style—Wolfe claims: "This had nothing to do with objectivity or subjectivity or taking a stand or 'commitment'—it was a matter of personality." For Wolfe, the most socially conservative New Journalist, these formal innovations have no radical substance other than the frisson of "experimenting with all the devices of realism, revving them up, trying to use them in a bigger way, with the full passion of innocents and discoverers." Of course, these devices were originally employed (at least in America) by novelists with a progressive social bent, which is probably why the children of Lincoln Steffens also called themselves New Journalists in the sixties. But so did Joan Didion, Gay Talese, Hunter Thompson, and Norman Mailer; this was a movement with many narrative stances.

Mailer's account of the Democratic convention that nominated John F. Kennedy, which had appeared in *Esquire* in 1961, rocked my assumptions about the boundary between fact and fiction, as did Talese's finely honed vignettes of life in Bay Ridge. Then there was Wolfe's criterion—his standard for a good story: the reader should come away marveling, "Do you believe people live like this?" It was enough to make a young writer abandon the dream of becoming a novelist. I began to write strange crossover essays, drifting in and out of the first person, and usually about the subject that obsessed me then: rock 'n' roll. I had always loved the music; even as an alienated adolescent taking refuge in Dos Passos and Salinger, I savored Dion and the Shirelles. To my mind, "jungle music" and "parajournalism" made a perfect fit: both were red-light districts of renegade sensibility—junk evolving into art. I could think of no better way to touch the music and describe the process by which it was rousing the sleeping giant of my generation than through prose that could incorporate the mythmaking power of fiction and the credibility of reportage.

After college, I went to journalism school, fascinated by the surreal syntax known as pyramid form. Here was a lurid yet minimal rhetoric that sought simultaneously to heighten and to reduce reality. It seemed thoroughly trad to me, but also utterly mod. My attempts to enrich the obit with Faulknerian melancholy did not sit well with the professors, nor did my lengthening hair, or the pieces about rock I infused with the breathless tropes of Tom Wolfe, who was then the Great Satan of journalism schools. "I don't know what this is," one professor scrawled across my copy, "but you owe me a story."

I owed him more than that, for after graduation, I landed a job at the *Voice*, bringing the entire "earning curve" of my class down. "I want to be a rock 'n' roll critic," I told Dan Wolfe, then the editor of the *Voice*. "What's that?" he slyly replied. It was 1966, and no one knew. I could make it up, invent a form and a persona, and in the process, re-create myself.

No publication today—not even the *Village Voice*—is run as the *Voice* was then. There was no editing to speak of, no stylebook, and barely any pay. At 6:00 a.m. on deadline day, tor-in-chief would arrive at the office, where, seated at me desks occupied by ad-takers from 9 to 5, writers had working all night, sustained by coffee and an occasional or nip. There were no story conferences or headline meetings, and the paper was laid out like wash on a line: pieces jumped forward and backward, sometimes several times. There was cunning to this chaos. It kept the overhead down, and it kept mediation at a minimum. The reader and the writer communicated as directly as print allowed, and this interplay of subjectivities was the ambition of the *Voice*. At its best, the paper operated on the assumption that only the amateur—fully sentient and willing to be involved—is fit to address the meaning of events. This romance of the individual had intricate ideological roots: it was what we had fought the Nazis for; why some of us stood up to red-baiters and racists, while others ran naked through the streets at dawn. But this was the sixties, when, as Frederic Jameson has written, "the 'natives' became fully human," and marginalities pushed front and center. For my (mostly white, ethnic, and male) cohort at the *Voice*, it was existentialism and roses. Our parents' struggles could be forgotten and their identities ignored. We were finally free to invent ourselves. The number one song in the whole United States said the answer was blowing in the wind.

In the end, we paid dearly for our naiveté, but for a time, it really seemed as if the old order was crumbling and each of us could expand to fill the void. Amid this shattering of boundaries—between classes, between genders, between personal and political experience—no one could say where the intellectual canon began and ended, and journalism, that old scavenger of forms, took on a giddy authority. This was no time for specialists: things were too unprecedented and unpredictable. To determine the meaning of a "happening" in which the actors urinated on the audience, a music that left the plane of all known tonality, or a political movement whose members tossed dollar bills down on the Stock Exchange—to decode all that would require a new openness, and a new style. It was left for the media to create that idiom, codifying concepts like "hip," "pop," and "revolution," so that they could be marketed. The Beatles were presiding over a new development in postindustrial culture—call it mass bohemianism. Hip-tabs like the *Voice* and, later, *Rolling Stone* were in a unique position to debunk this hype while profiting from it. And profit they did.

Hip journalists, for the most part, did not grow rich. We had adventures, not assets; and when the police decided reporters were agents of the enemy within, we took it on the chin. At the *Voice*, there was a collection of press cards on a wall behind the editor's desk, each flecked with gore. One of these cards belonged to our consciousness correspondent, a tender fellow named Don McNeill, who'd been covering a Youth International Party (or Yippie) demonstration when the police rammed his head through a plate glass door. By 1968, reporters had learned to take off their credentials during demos, for safety's sake. But there were other, less riveting reminders that the countercultural bubble was about to burst. The promise of rock music—its vision of a multiracial community of the young—had been subverted by a record industry bloated on profit. The same entrepreneurial feeding frenzy had reduced the psychedelic experience to dayglo chatchkas, while its gurus scurried for the shelter of their wealth, remote from the battle-grounds of civil rights and Vietnam. Our faith in individualism was proving to be the ultimate marketable commodity.

As it became apparent that hip was fuel for the engines of an expansionist economy, it was more and more difficult to write about the counterculture apart from its co-optation. My work began to focus on this process, as it sucked in activists along with rock stars. The pseudo event became my beat, and the tone of my column—which I'd named "Pop Eye"—changed from irony to confusion, pain, and rage. I knew the music and the movement meant something to their followers, but the closer one got to the hot center, the more this revolution resembled spectacle for the sake of publicity. And I was much too close to maintain the tone of amused elation Tom Wolfe had perfected in his pieces about the California teenage Regency. Time and time again, I watched the struggle to assert com-munity collapse in the face of fortunes to be made. And the more I tried to evoke this vortex, the more caught up in it I became. In the same week Don McNeill's baffled, bloody face appeared on page one of the *Voice*, I had dinner with a Broadway producer who tried to convince me to write the book for a musical called *I Protest!* Meanwhile, my agent was out to market me as a talk-show team with Rocky Graziano. I couldn't handle the contradictions, and withdrew into a rigid terror, all too easily mistaken for sixties cool.

Then came the assassinations of 1968 and their explosive aftermath I was shot at and teargassed during the Democratic Convention in Chicago. A few months before, I'd leapt from a second-story window at Columbia University, as club-wielding cops broke down the dormitory doors. These events shattered the ethic of insulation I'd been taught in journalism school. But they also forced me to question the imperatives of New Journalism. I could no longer regard the writer as the hero of every story. The more I felt implicated in my subject, the less I felt entitled to intrude. In 1970, I was assigned to cover the trial of Angela Davis, a young black professor who'd been accused of helping a convict named George Jackson to escape. I had a series of pieces, maybe even a book, in mind; this was my chance for a major career move. Then the trial began. At a hearing in San Francisco, I sat next to Jackson's mother. Her youngest son had been killed during the failed escape attempt, and her eldest now sat chained in a chair bolted to the floor. I had seen that several times in American courtrooms—always when a black man was on trial. But this time, something beyond imagining (even then) occurred: the lights went out. In the darkness, I heard Jackson screaming. He was being beaten to a pulp by guards who claimed he was trying to escape. I will never forget the sound of that beating or the look on his mother's face—and I would never write the book I'd planned. I filed only one piece on Angela Davis: a pastiche of news clips and interviews, seething with suppressed rage. In the end, the style I had constructed seemed utterly inadequate to the task of expressing what I felt: the intense empathy toward my subject, the contempt for a system that had proven itself every bit as lawless as its criminals, and the alienation that comes of loathing your own.

With the rise of Nixon's silent majority, the counterculture fell into a numb silence, and I was writing about suburban marches against hunger, in the pinched tones of a weary ironist. Events like that struck me as a signature of the end of the sixties, a grand metaphor for co-opting social change. The Hip Community was about to shrink dramatically, and with it, the intermingling of mass and elite forms. It wasn't long before most New Journalists had returned to fiction, and the few who remained made peace with the tabs.

In the 20-odd years since I wrote the pieces in this collection, American journalism has changed a great deal. Though literary devices still crop up in reportage, the narrator is nearly always an impersonal presence, and on those rare occasions when the first person intrudes, it must stand for the reader's fantasy: "We're sitting in a holding pen, the killer and I." Sensibility is nearly absent from mainstream media—consider the shift in affect from Murrow to Koppel—and down in the trenches of trash TV, the only permissible persona is that of a right-wing haranguer who enforces the consensus. No one in journalism dares to doubt. As the profession toughens up, and the outlets for eccentricity tighten up, it becomes harder and harder to imagine a personal rhetoric of popular dissent. This is the most urgent reason to exhume the artifacts of New Journalism: its techniques were refined at the moment when we first began to grapple with the power of mass media to standardize experience, and its embrace of subjectivity was an attempt to resist this processed consensus. Such issues are with us still, as we struggle to build community and assert the distinction between culture and commodity. And the central premise of New Journalism—that the individual is the true register of events—seems as urgent now, in this age of thought control by death threat, as it did 20 years ago, when I set out to report the counterculture for the *Village Voice*. Subjectivity is still a subversive act.

REPORTING
THE COUNTERCULTURE

PART I

The Music

CHAPTER 1

Gear

Too early to get up, especially on Saturday. The sun peeks over his windowsill. Isolated footsteps from the street. Guys who have to work on Saturday. Boy! That's what they'll call you all your life if you don't stay in school. Forty-five definitions, two chapters in *Silas Marner*, and three chem labs. On Sunday night, he will sit in his room with the radio on, bobbing back and forth on his bed, opening the window wide and then closing it, taking a break to eat, to comb his hair, to dance, to hear the Stones—anything. Finally, cursing wildly and making ugly faces at himself in the mirror, he will throw *Silas Marner* under the bed and spend an hour watching his tortoise eat lettuce.

In the bathroom, he breaks three screaming pimples. With a toothpick, he removes four specks of food from his braces, skirting dangerously barbed wires and week-old rubber bands. Brooklyn Bridge, railroad tracks, they called them. Metal mouth. They said he was skinny. They said he smiled like someone was holding a gun to his head. Bent fingers with filthy nails. Caved-in chest with eight dangling hairs. A face that looks like the end of a watermelon and curly hair—not like the Stones, not at all like Brian Jones, but muddy curls running down his forehead and over his ears. A bump, smashed by a bat thrown wildly into his future when he was eight, a hunchback Quasimodo Igor on his head. A bump. Nobody hip has a bump or braces. Or hair like a fucking Frankenstein movie. He licks his braces clean and practices smiling.

Hair straight and heavy. Nose full. Lips bulging like boiling frankfurters. Hung. Bell bottoms and boss black boots. He practices his Brian Jones expressions. Fist held close to the jaw.

3

Ready to spring, ready to spit. Evil. His upper brace catches on a lip.

Ronnie walks past his parents' bedroom, where his mother sleeps in a gauzy hairnet, the covers pulled over her chin, her baby feet exposed and yellowed by calluses. Her hand reaches over to the night table, where her eyedrops and glasses lay. Ronnie mutters silently at her. The night before, there had been a fight—the usual fight, with Mommy shouting, "I'll give you money . . . sure . . . you rotten kid . . . I'll give you clothing so you can throw it all over the floor ... that's blood money in those pants of yours." And him answering the usual "geh-awf-mah-bak," and her: "Don't you yell at me, don't you . . . did you hear that [to no one] . . . did you hear that kid . . . and him slamming the door—the gray barrier—and above the muffled ". . . disrespects his mother . . . he treats me like dirt under his feet . . . he'll spit on my grave . . ." and finally Dad's groaning shuffle and a murmured: "Ronnie, you better shut your mouth to your mother," and him whispering, silently, the climactic, the utter: "Fucking bitch. Cunt. Cunt."

He doesn't know why he cursed, except that she did not like it. It was easy to make her cry. Though he shivers at the thought of her lying across the bed sobbing into a pillow, her housedress pulled slightly over a varicose thigh, he has to admit it was easy.

On the table he sees the pants she bought him yesterday. Her money lining his pocket, he had taken the bus to Fordham Road, and in Alexander's he had searched out the Mod rack. Hands shaking, dying for a cigarette, he found the pants—a size small but still a fit. He bought them, carried them home clutched in his armpit, and deposited them before her, during prime *Man from UNCLE* time.

"Get away, I can't see. Whatsamadduh, your father a glacier or something?" And when he unveiled the pants and asked for the usual cuff-making ritual (when he would stand on the ladder and she, holding a barrage of pins in her mouth, ran the tailor's chalk along his shoe line and made him drag out the old black sewing machine), the fight had begun—and ended within the hour. The pants, sewn during *The Merv Griffin Show* as the last labor of the night, now lay exposed and sunlit on the table—$8.95 pants.

4

They shimmer. The houndstooth design glows against the formica. Brown and green squares are suddenly visible within the gray design. He brushes the fabric carefully so the wool bristles. He tries them on, zipping up the two-inch fly, thinking at first that he has broken the zipper until he realizes that hip huggers have no fly to speak of. They buckle tightly around his hips, hug his thighs, and flare suddenly at the knees. He races to the mirror and grins.

His hips are suddenly tight and muscular. His waist is sleek and his ass round and bulging. Most important, the pants make him look hung. Like the kids in the park. The odor of stale cigarettes over their clothing. Crucifixes dangling out of their shirts. Belt buckles ajar. They are hip. They say, "Check out dat bike." Get bent on Gypsy. Write the numbers of cruising police cars all over the walls. In the park, they buzz out on glue, filling their paper bags and breathing deeply, then falling back on the grassy slopes, watching the cars. Giggling. Grooving. High.

Sometimes they let him keep the models that come with the glue. Or he grubs around their spot until, amid the torn bags and oozing tubes, he finds a Messerschmitt or Corvair spread across the grass in ruins, as though it had crashed there.

He unzips the pants and lets them hang on the door, where he can watch them from the living room. He takes a box of Oreos from the kitchen, stacking the cookies in loose columns on the rug. He pours a cup of milk and turns on the TV. Farmer Gray runs nervously up and down the screen while a pig squats at ease by his side. His pants are filled with hornets. He runs in a cloud of dust toward a pond that appears and disappears teasingly, leaving Farmer Gray grubbing in the sand. Cut down.

He fills his mouth with three Oreos and wraps his feet around the screen so he can watch Farmer Gray between his legs. Baby habit. Eating cookies on the floor and watching cartoons on Saturday morning. Baby habit, Mommy called it. Like thumbsucking. They teased him about it until he threw imaginary furniture into their faces. A soft bulge on his left thumb from years of sucking. Cost them a fortune in braces. Always busting his hump.

He kills the TV picture, and puts the radio on softly, because he doesn't want to wake Dad, who is asleep on his cot in the middle of the living room, bunched up around the blanket, his face creased in a dream, hands gripping his stomach in mock tension. Dad snores regularly, in soft growls.

He brushes a flock of Oreo crumbs under the TV, and rubs a milk stain into the rug. Thrown out of your own bed for snoring. You feel cheap; like Little Bo Peep; beep beep beep beep.

Maybe he should go downstairs. The guys are out already, slung over cars and around lampposts. The girls are trickling out of the project. It's cloudy, but until it actually rains he knows they will be around the lamppost, spitting into the street, horsing around, grubbing for hooks, singing. He finishes four more cookies and stuffs half an apple onto his chocolate-lined tongue.

Marie Giovanni put him down bad for his braces. When she laughs, her tits shake. Her face is pink; her hair rises in a billowing bouffant. In the hallway, she let Tony get his fingers wet. Yesterday, she cut on him: called him metal mouth.

He flicks the radio shut, grabs the pants, and slides into them. He digs out a brown poor-boy sweater from under a rubble of twisted clothing (they dress him like a ragpicker) and shines his boots with spit. The heels are worn down on one side, but they make him look an inch taller, so he wears them whenever he can.

He combs his hair in the mirror. Back on the sides, over the ears, over the eyes to cover up his bump. Straight down the back of his neck, so it rests on his collar. He checks his bald spot for progress and counts the hairs that come out in his brush. In two years, he's convinced he'll be bald in the front and his bump will look like a boulder on his forehead.

He sits on his bed and turns the radio on. From under the phonograph, he lifts a worn fan magazine—*Pop* in bright fuchsia lettering, with Zal Yanovsky hunched over one P, Paul McCartney contorted over the other, and Brenda Lee touching her toes around the O. He turns to a spread on the Stones, and flips the pages until he sees The Picture. Mick Jagger and Crissie Shrimpton. Mick scowling, waving his fingers in the air. Crissie watching the camera. Crissie waiting for the photographer to shoot. Crissie. Crissie. Eyes fading brown circles, lips slightly parted in flashbulb surprise, miniskirt spread apart, tits like two perfect cones under her sweater. He had to stop looking at Crissie Shrimpton a week ago.

6

He turns the page and glances at the shots of Brian Jones, and then his eyes open wide because a picture in the corner shows Brian in Ronnie's pants. The same check. The same rise and flare. Brian leaning against a wall, his hands on the waist of his magic hip huggers. Wiiicked.

He flips the magazine away and stands in a curved profile against the mirror. He watches the pants move as he does. From a nearby flowerpot he gathers a fingerful of dirt and rubs it over his upper lip, moustache-style. He checks hair, nose, braces, nails, and pants. He likes the pants. They make him look hung. He reaches into his top drawer and pulls out a white handkerchief. He opens his fly and inserts the rolled cloth, patting it in place, and closing the zipper over it. He looks bosssss.

In the elevator, Ronnie takes a cigarette from his three-day-old pack and keeps it unlit in his mouth. Marie Giovanni will look at his pants and giggle. Tony will bellow, "Check out dem pants," and everyone will groove on him. In the afternoon, they will take him down to the park and turn him on and he will feel the buzz they are always talking about and the cars speeding by like sparklers.

Brian Jones thoughts in his head. Tuff thoughts. He will slouch low over the car, and smoke with his thumb over the cigarette—the hip way. And when he comes back upstairs, they will finally get off his back. And even on Fordham Road, where the Irish kids crack up when he walks by, even in chemistry and gym, they will know who he is and nod a soft "hey" when he comes by. He'll get laid.

Because clothing IS important. Especially if you've got braces and bony fingers and a bump the size of a goddam coconut on your head.

And especially if you're 14. Because—ask anyone—14 is shit.

—1966

CHAPTER 2

Shango Mick Arrives

NEW YORK—The African god of thunder landed in New York City last Thursday afternoon.

Shango came wrapped in the steel body of a TWA jetliner, from the land of the new vinyl gods, London. At the airport that afternoon, Shango-worshipers stood tense and sweating along the open observation deck. Their binoculars were poised. Their Polaroid Swingers said, "YES!"

The jet landed amid a churning blast of mechanical thunder. The portable staircase was fixed in place. The stewardesses departed. Finally, the Godheads: Charlie first, then Bill and Keith. Then Brian, who removed his purple glasses to survey the scene, and wiped them on his candy-cane blazer. Finally, Mick, smiling lamely, somehow supported by the brass-button epaulets on his shoulders. The young gods descended and posed.

For those who have no children, whose radio dials are stuck on FM, or whose television sets are broken, their names are Bill Wyman, Charlie Watts, Keith Richard, Brian Jones, and Mick Jagger. Their "approximate" age is 21. Their gross for this year may exceed $8 million. Their hard-rock sound is a curry of straight sex, destruction, repulsion, and hip—all garnished with a pseudo-blues accent and spiced with Oriental chord progressions. We are not nice, but we are honest, says the image. We are not respectable, but we are real.

These five guys, and their manager, Andrew Loog Oldham, call themselves the Rolling Stones.

• • •

Everybody here? Photographers, fashion models, record executives, flacks, a few disheveled reporters, and a stray groupie who is hustled off the field screaming, "Keith—Keeeth?"

Out on the field, we watch the plane circle and descend. A promo man tells us what they're really like:

"Pigs. They're pigs. I nearly caught one of them in the head last year. Told him to put his hand on the rail and he said, 'Fuck you, man.' Keith Richard. And he's supposed to be the nice one."

"Lovely people," a cop chimes in. "Last year a couple of girls broke through and touched them. We had to vaccinate them. You never saw so much smeared makeup. Jesus."

A free-lance photographer says he'd rather be up at Yankee Stadium with the baseball players. "They show you some respect; they ask about the family."

And an airport porter advises: "They're down. Good luck. And remember the 15-foot business. Otherwise, you're contaminated."

● ● ●

EXCERPT FROM A CONVERSATION WITH MISS BETSY DOSTER, PRESS INFORMATION FOR THE STONES, PURSUANT TO A PRIVATE INTERVIEW: "No."

ITEM FROM THE JAN/66 ISSUE OF RAVE MAGAZINE: "Basically every pop singer is normal (despite what many say) and at times the hurdy-gurdy life of being continuously in the public eye is too much for anyone . . . Trying to be nice to everyone no matter what they say or do is sometimes too much."

FURTHER PERSPECTIVE FROM A FORMER PROMO MAN FOR THE STONES: "They go on the theory that a knock is a boost. No matter what they do, it's the Stones. If a clean image group acted that way, they'd be finished. Suits, brawls, evictions—it's all part of the Stones' cool."

INSIGHT FROM A WRITER ON POP, AN ACQUAINTANCE, A FAN: "Mick belched in the middle of a press conference. It was the biggest belch in the world and he didn't say anything at all."

● ● ●

From the corner of my eye, a large cardboard poster steals its way across the field. A protest? A Beatle plot? No; it's the cover of *Town and Country*—Stones meet society—blown up and transplanted to a 15-foot slab. Two fashion editors grasp the tribute and try to maneuver it into the customs area, where the Stones are being processed. But the cops stop them, so they park it on the hood of a limousine, where the boys will be sure to see it.

I wander over to customs. Handymen and porters gape and gawk from the windows. At the door, they are commenting on those filthy, fruity kids inside. Since I'm wearing a police press card, I'm a real reporter for the day; the cops let me through. I yell: "Press, Press," and suddenly I'm facing the Stones. They are jumping around, hollering, scowling. Bill and Mick are laughing hysterically. Charlie is signing an autograph for a porter who has doubtless refused to move the group's instruments until a page is inscribed for his daughter.

Brian is standing alone. He turns and catches me snapping a contraband picture. He removes his shades, and those evil eyes begin to stare. It's a put-down look. I know it from MacDougal Street. So I stare back. But the expression on Brian's face is puzzlement. He seems to be saying: "What are you doing in dirty jeans and long hair taking a picture of me with a professional reporter's credentials?" And I'm staring back, saying: "Brian, why do they call you a god of destruction when you're just a kid jumping around making money and trouble? And Brian, are you ever frightened when those tiny feminine nails begin to scratch on your hotel door? And what's it like in those alone moments when the guitar is unplugged and the clothes come off and you're standing there in naked mufti?"

So we stare at each other, and I snap my picture to break the spell and Brian puts his shades back on and scowls.

● ● ●

A FAN FROM MEMPHIS TELLS HIT PARADER MAGAZINE THAT THEY'RE REALLY HOMEY-TYPE GUYS: "I thought they were very nice and courteous, the very opposite to all the rumors I'd heard because everyone told me they were gonna be real rude and wouldn't want to talk to me."

A BRITISH JOURNALIST SAYS TALKING TO THE STONES IS LIKE GOING TO THE DENTIST. "A few 'fab gear whacks' and a little 'in' patter which you cannot possibly share in will reduce reporters to stuttering, embarrassed heaps."

● ● ●

NEW YORK, June 24—The Rolling Stones, a prominent British pop-music singing group, held an informal press reception

11

on their rented yacht, Sea Panther, today. The five musicians are being quartered on the 112-foot craft during their current American tour because hotel officials have refused to grant them reservations. They are currently suing 14 New York hotels in the dispute.

The reception began as the yacht departed from the 79th Street Boat Basin. All the Stones were present, and their manager, Andrew Loog Oldham, enthusiastically held forth amid a cluster of reporters. A buffet luncheon was served.

The group was splendidly attired in their distinctive style. Mick Jagger, lead vocalist, wore a striped double-breasted blazer and white bell-bottom slacks. Songwriter Keith Richard wore an epaulet shirt and red suede boots. And guitarist Brian Jones placed a button, "Sex is here to stay," on the fly of his white, wide-wale corduroys."

—spiked on the city desk at the *New York Times*

• • •

A LYRICAL INTERLUDE: "You're the kind of person you meet at certain dismal dull affairs/You say how the crowd is much too loud running up and down the stairs/Well it seems to me that you have sinned too much in too few years/And though you try you just can't hide/Your eyes are filled with tears."

—"Nineteenth Nervous Breakdown"

The motors churn and the yacht begins to move. Mick says: "It's 95 out and you'd never know it here." Charlie says: "Don't let those photographers make you nervous; ask your questions." Keith says efforts to censor rock songs because of their subject matter is "typicow American prudery." Brian says: "The next thing in pop won't happen for another three years." And Andrew says: " 'Satisfaction' is our national anthem."

The press meets/versus the Rolling Stones. A starry-eyed reporter for the *New York Post* follows Andrew around, scrawling dutifully on a worn pad. Those ladies from *Town and Country* are back with their publicity blowup. The boys pose and the ladies smile, their jobs secure until the next invasion. WMCA good-guy Gary Stevens, in a blue pinstripe suit, chortles: "Hey, Keith Baby, how about we do a tape? We do a tape, huh?" So Keith smiles lamely and says: "Sure, Gary." And Charlie sits, yawns, and smokes cigarettes.

Meanwhile, Mick is responding to a question from some radio reporter: "What's the difference between the Stones and the Beatles?"

"There are five of us and four of them. That's the difference."

And Brian stares at the passing Statue of Liberty, pulls out a red handkerchief, and waves it in the general direction of the bronze lady.

"Who are more uncooperative, Brian? British or American journalists?"

"We're the ones who are uncooperative, right mate?"

• • •

THE ART DIRECTOR OF A FAN MAGAZINE GASPS AT BRIAN JONES'S BEHAVIOR: "I was taking pictures of him at a discotheque and he walked right up to me, stuck out his chest, and said: 'I wouldn't do that again, mate.' I really thought he was going to hit me."

A POP WRITER COMPARES THE OLD AND NEW STONES: "I think now there's a feeling of—don't touch me, I'm a Rolling Stone. Andrew is so hung up on himself, it's unbelievable. He's a hippy in the true sense of the word. When someone says something honest, he goes blank. He can't relate to honesty."

MICK JAGGER EVALUATED: "Everyone thinks he's completely out of it, but he's got his own perception of things. He lives up to the Stones' image, but sometimes when he says hippy things, he flushes."

• • •

You are sitting next to Mick, but he defies approach. The others are shorter, pudgier, softer than they sound on record. But Mick really looks and sounds like Shango. A while ago, he was hospitalized, suffering from "nervous exhaustion." Now, you watch him smiling, chatting, trying to respond. You watch him "circulate." You watch his tired grin, his oval eyes and sagging lips, and his brightly colored yachtsman outfit becomes an irony. You want to ask: "Mick, how the hell are you going to manage concerts in 29 cities in 27 days?" You want to say: "Mick tell me what the business is really like. Tell me about payola. Talk about under-assistant West Coast promo men. What's it like working your ass off recording, performing, posing, chatting. How does $8 million feel? Does Ed Sullivan have bad breath?"

But you can't do that at a press reception, on a yacht circling Manhattan Island. You can't really know or even guess what it's like to be a Rolling Stone with diarrhea or hay fever. You want to touch Mick Jagger? You can't even come close.

• • •

LYRICAL DIVERSION AND PREGNANT PAUSE: When I'm riding round the world/And I'm doing this and I'm signing that/And I'm trying to make some girl/Who tells me, baby better come back/Maybe next week . . . /I can't get no satisfaction/No no no/Hey hey hey.

• • •

Ashore, 200 girls shriek as the Rolling Stones leave their yacht. Six policemen cordon off a route to the underground garage where the limousine is parked, doors ajar. The Stones, stern-faced and braced for a riot, walk into the waiting police arms, but the girls are too clever for New York's Finest. They break the lines and rush the group. The Stones scurry madly into the cavernous garage. Everyone makes it except Brian, who is engulfed in lips and fingernails. A shrieking hand pulls his hair. Something snags his lip. Five girls clutch at his jacket and pants. Twilight of the gods. Brian is pale and helpless. Sacrificial wailing. The reporters form a flying wedge and begin to pull the fans from Brian's back. Finally he climbs inside, while a girl screams after him: "I got a hair!" The car takes off, but not before the kamikaze groupies throw themselves over the hood and into its path. The garage explodes in shrieks of brakes and ecstasy. Real tears are shed. Hands are quivering as the car pulls away.

Outside, an African sun shines over the Sea Panther. Muffled sound of drumbeats from the river. Burst of thunder from the motors. And a girl with merging freckles asks: "Dijuh touch him? Dijuh touch Mick?"

—1966

CHAPTER 3

Next Year in San Francisco

PHILADELPHIA—Tonight's crowd ambles languidly across the floor of the Electric Factory, a huge garage turned psychedelic playground. Mostly, they're straight kids come to gape at the hippies and fathom the Now. Ten years ago, they would have preened their pompadours before the cameras on *American Bandstand*. Today, they steal furtive drags on filter-tip cigarettes, trying to look high. They've all had their palms read by the wizard in the balcony, and their faces painted in the adjacent boutique. Now, they stand like limp meringue, watching a local group called Edison's Electric Machine belt out the psychedelic jive.

A real death scene. Not a pleasant sight for Janis, who peers through a crack in the dressing room door, and scowls, "Oh shit. We'll never be able to get into those kids. Want to see death? Take a look out there. You ever played Philadelphia? No, of course not. You don't *play* anywhere."

You could say she gets nervous before a set. The other members of Big Brother and the Holding Company sit guzzling beer, trying on beads, and hassling their roadie. But Janis stalks around the tiny room, her fingers drumming against a tabletop. She sips hot tea from a Styrofoam cup. She talks in gasps, and between sentences she belts down Southern Comfort. That brand is her trademark. Tonight, a knowing admirer has graced her dressing room with a fifth, in lieu of flowers. "I don't drink anything on the rocks," she explains. "Cold is bad for my throat. So, it's always straight or in tea. Tastes like orange petals in tea. I usually get about a pint and a half down me when I'm performing. Any more, I start to nod out."

Now, the B-group files in, dripping sweat. The lead singer gingerly places his guitar in its plush casket, and peels off an imitation brocade jacket, sweatshirt, pullover, and soaked undershirt. "Why do you wear all that clothing if it's so hot out there?" Janis asks.

"Because I'm freaky." And the door opens again to admit a fully attired gorilla with rubber hands and feet. Janis glances briefly at the ground to make sure it's still there, and then offers the gorilla some booze. He lifts his mask to accept. His name is Gary the Gorilla, and Janis digs that, so she gives him her bottle to hold during the set, and follows Peter the bassman through the dressing room door. Gary unzips his belly and passes his feet around, and the lead singer of Edison's Electric Machine examines a rip in his brocade, consoling himself with the B-group's prayer: Next Year in San Francisco.

• • •

I first met them last year in San Francisco. In a ranch house with an unobstructed view of ticky tack. They were assembled for an interview on hippie culture, and I began with a nervous question about turning on. In answer, somebody lit up and soon the floor was hugging-warm. I glanced down at my notes as though they had become hieroglyphics (which they had). When it was time to split, and everyone had boarded a paisley hearse, I muttered something like, "We shouldn't be interviewed. We should be friends." And the car drove away laughing, with long hair flying from every window.

This summer, 20,000 nomads will be on Haight Street, hoping to get discovered like Janis, in some psychedelic Schwab's. But I'm afraid Big Brother and the Holding Company is the last of the great San Francisco bands. With new groups trying on art music like training bras, they are a glorious throwback to a time when the primary aim in rock was "to get people moving"—nothing more or less. They were nurtured in the hippie renaissance: played the Trips Festival and the first productions of the Family Dog; jammed together in a big house at 1090 Page Street, a mecca for musicians back when the only interested talent scouts were cops.

In 1961, Janis and Chet Helms (proprietor of the Family Dog) hitchhiked west. They were anonymous freaks then, newly plucked from Texas topsoil. "What were the two of you like then, Janis?"

"Oh—younger."

"How were you different from today?"

"We were . . . umm . . . just interested in being beatniks then. Now, we've got responsibilities, and I guess you could say, ambition."

She was born in Port Arthur, Texas, in 1943. Dropped out of four or five schools. Sang in hillbilly bars with a local blue-grass band. For the beer. "We'd do country songs, and then the band'd shut up and I'd sing blues, 'cause that was my thing."

Her thing was no Patti Page regatta, no Connie Francis sob-along, but a mangy backwoods blues, heavy with devotion to Bessie Smith. She still smears Bessie across everything she sings, making it possible for a whole generation of us to hear beyond the scratches in those old records. But she says she never really tried to sing rock until she joined Big Brother.

"See, Bessie, she sang big open notes in very simple phrasing. But you can't fall back on that in front of a rock band. I mean, you can't sing loose and easy with a throbbing amplifier and drums behind you. The beat just pushes you on. So I started singing rhythmically, and now I'm learning from Otis Redding to push a song instead of just sliding over it."

It was Chet Helms who made Janis part of the Holding Company (before that, it had been an instrumental band, one of dozens formed during the merger of folk, jazz, and rock among Bay Area youth). From the start their music began to clothe her voice. They taught her to blast, pound, and shatter a song. She returned the favor by directing her solos toward the group's rhythmic heart.

"I have three voices," she explains. "The shouter; the husky, guttural chick; and the high wailer. When I turn into a nightclub singer, I'll probably use my husky voice. That's the one my mother likes. She says, 'Janis, why do you scream like that when you've got such a pretty voice?' "

It's not a pretty sound she makes now. A better word would be "primal." She plants herself onstage like a firmly rooted tree, then whips more emotion out of her upper branches than most singers can wring out of their lower depths. She stings like sunburn, shrieks like war. And she does one other thing that makes it all so sexy. She needs. Needs to move, to feel, to be screamed at; needs to touch and be touched.

" 'Ball And Chain' is the hardest thing I do. I have to really get inside my head, every time I sing it. Because it's about feeling things. That means, I can never sing it without really trying. See, there's this big hole in the song that's mine, and I've got to fill it with something. So, I do. And it really tires me out. But, it's so groovy when you know the audience really wants you. I mean, whatever you give them, they'll believe in. And they yell back at you, call your name and like that."

It's always the same: at Monterey, where the media discovered her; at the Avalon in San Francisco, where they know her best; at the Anderson, where the New York press corps first saw her perform; and tonight at the Electric Factory in Philadelphia. She begs and coaxes her audiences until they begin to holler, first in clichés like "do-it-to-it" and finally in wordless squeals. Suddenly, the room is filled with the agony in her voice. Kids surround the stage, spilling over with the joy of having been reached. Even nerds in neckties nod their heads and whisper, "Shit . . . oh shit." Because to hear Janis sing "Ball and Chain" just once is to have been laid, lovingly and well.

● ● ●

Two sets later, they are back in the dressing room, flushed with sweat and applause. There is another hassle with the roadie. Dave the drummer changes into his third shirt that evening. And Janis is sitting on Gary the Gorilla's lap, fondling his furry knees and opening a second fifth of Southern Comfort.

"Why do I always hafta dance alone in these places?" she rasps. "I mean, you saw me dancing out there between sets. All those guys were standing around, panting in the corner. Finally, I had to say to one of 'em: 'Well, do you wanna dance, or not?' and he comes on waving his arms around like a fuckin' bat. Didn't even look at me. Now, why do things like that always happen?"

"Because you're so weird looking, Janis," the roadie answers.

She nods slowly, and whispers, "Yeah." She digs and detests her weirdness. She would like to be the freakiest chick in rock,

18

and a gracious young lady as well. At a recent press party, to celebrate the group's new contract with Columbia Records, Janis shook out her hair only to confront a lady out of *Harper's Bazaar* who covered up her drink and said, "Do you mind?" "Fuck off, baby," Janis replied. But later she was seen pouting before a mirror, muttering, "Face it, baby, you've got ratty hair."

Now she moves out of the tiny room and surveys the remnants of this evening's scene: cigarette butts and a gaggle of local freaks. Peter the bassman is already making contact with a pale young lady searching for a seminal autograph. And Gandalf, the wizard from the balcony, offers to read every palm in the room, whispering, "Hey—let's go up to your room and smoke."

Later, at a hamburger stand, Gandalf stops in the middle of a poem he is composing on a napkin and reflects: "Tomorrow, I'm gonna make it with Janis. I'm gonna just go up to her and say 'Hey—let's make it.' 'Cause she's so groovy to watch. What a bod she must have under that voice." He pauses to consider it, and then asks a waitress for spare whipped cream cans.

But Gandalf the wizard may have to wait longer than tomorrow. For this very night, while Philadelphia sleeps, Janis is with Gary the Gorilla, and they are finishing off the second fifth. Together.

—1968

CHAPTER 4

Harlequin in Neon

LAS VEGAS—Flight 711 coasts into Las Vegas at twilight, when the desert sky is flecked with color-dust. Neon sparkles everywhere. Whole streets move at stroboscopic speed. Buildings blink and twirl like colossal blossoms of light. The very air seems charged with a dry electric musk.

Vegas is the fake-crystal chandelier in the American pleasure dome, and the biggest bauble of all is Caesar's Palace. As the taxi glides past the hotel (150 feet of floodlit fountains in a garden of pseudoclassic statuary), my eyes are assaulted by a Cinerama billboard that proclaims its message in letters 7 feet high: TINY TIM.

America's current curio-in-residence, a Quasimodo to the middle classes, is appearing twice nightly in the Circus Maximus Room, amid the jangle of rhinestones and currency. Harlequin in neon; he's right up there, immortalized beside the topless earth-mother-a-go-go. Local newspapers are filled with planted items about his eccentricities. You can't avoid his iridescent falsetto on the radio. Souvenir stands hawk decals with his name embossed. And tourists brandish plastic tulips in his honor.

Nothing can stop a freak whose time has come. And this is Tiny's moment. With death and damnation cluttering the news, Johnny Carson can count on a knowing snicker from his audience when he mutters, "Tiny Tim kills bugs dead." (Get it? Flit!) Now, when crowds tire of shtick about ungrateful kids and spiteful mothers-in-law, there is always Tiny Tim. "Have you heard, he's entering the Miss

America pageant?" goes the routine. "He's representing Death Valley."

Tiny himself is less than delighted with his role as show-biz scapegoat. Under the cosmetic camp, he sees himself as a wandering minstrel. His aim may be nostalgic, but his immediate effect is comic. Tiny is not the first troubadour to survive by playing the clown, but his successes have been so interlaced with ridicule that he has come to value mockery the way most performers dig applause.

"This clown role is something I've always lived with," he admits. "In the old days, they didn't want legitimate singing from me. I was hired strictly as a novelty. But nothing mattered more to me than selling my songs. Even today, that's true. If they think of me as a harlequin, that doesn't bother me, as long as they appreciate what I sing."

Ah, but they love it. At the slot machines, they chant his name like a mantra. In a supersnack bar called the Noshorium, a spangle-ridden matron clutches tulips to her breast and warbles, "Let's see Tiny Tim. He's my favorite freak." Beautiful people adore him for his chic; ugly people find him more stimulating than the Three Stooges. The underground worships his saintly cool, while the mainstream is dazzled by his market potential. Kids shine in his presence, as though he were a prince out of Hans Christian Andersen. And bevies of boppers are dying to be the first in their tract developments to make Tiny Tim.

Before his canonization by Johnny Carson, I used to watch him warm up crowds at the Scene, a rock cellar off Times Square. He'd stand there, his cheeks aglow in the discoglare. The floor around him was alive with buttocks (because in Times Square, they dance with only their hips). In some damp and darkened corner, I would always spot some chick cracking up over his makeup. Of course, I hadn't known him as Larry Love or Derry Dover, I'd never seen him play a freak show on Eighth Avenue or a tourist trap in the Village. I certainly hadn't even caught him singing on the subways, when there was no other gig to be had. He was just another dissociated gnome to me, and watching him perform, I couldn't shake the impression that he was laying bare his soul to ridicule and anticipating the result. That scene frightened me, always has.

Three years and superstardom have done little to change his act or diminish my fear. So I proceed with caution toward the Atrium Room, where Tiny is holding a reception for his "dear friends" from the press. Ahead of me, a burly local with a string tie bisecting his Adam's apple shouts, "There he is. By gosh, I thought he was colored."

Inside, I spot Tiny right away, leaning against the marbleized wallpaper, in a baggy black raincoat. It distinguishes him from his retinue of tailored hairlines and suppressed waists. These promo-men take turns squiring Tiny around the floor. The whole ritual is danced like a pallid minuet. Tiny curtsies with his wrist and performs a short, sprinting twirl. But his smile is frozen in place, and in his eyes I notice a deep tinge of exhaustion.

The underground press has been full of stories about Tiny Tim mesmerized by his managers. But I've never been able to buy that myth. Performers are victimized by their own desire, and they find surrogates to shoulder the blame. I offer in evidence Richard Perry, the 26-year-old producer who has masterminded Tiny's current success. Perry first met his client in 1965, when Tiny was taking the door-to-door route to obscurity. "I took one look at him and classified him as another Tin Pan Alley freak," Perry explains. "But then he started to sing—you know, standing there with his ukulele. And my mind was shattered. I took him back to my office and just sat there for hours recording him."

Perry has seen Tiny come a long way since then. Every inch the proud guardian, he watches Tiny out of the corner of his drink while I question him about the show. It is going over well, though its star is still nervous about all those dancing girls. "He looks a little . . . uncomfortable," I prod. Perry stares into the fizzy depths of his drink. "Well," he whispers, "he's still getting adjusted to his new environment."

● ● ●

Nineteen fifty-eight was a smug, clean-shaven year in anyone's book. But for Herberto Buckingham Kaury, it must have been hell in small doses. He moved through the streets of Upper Manhattan with his makeup and his shopping bag. The kids called him Crazy Herbie and celebrated his every appearance with a hail of abuse. With his dishrag hair and his face like a demolished Edsel, he was ugly as sin. And in 1958, ugly *was* sin.

But he resisted (out of psychic need, if not pride) and his protest took the form of protective fantasy. He built a wall of nostalgia around his mind, filtering all external experience through a rosy haze of recollections. The raw material for his collage came from those classic havens for the tormented, movies and music. Others may have looked upon him as an outcast, but he saw himself as a wind chime, held against the breeze of memory.

"I used to close the door to hear my records," he recalls. "I had to be alone, in the dark, because then I could feel I was in the phonograph with the singers, feeling their voices inside me. And it was the same with movies. I always went alone. I'd see six movies a day—from twelve noon till twelve at night. Films about the 1890s or early 1900s I'd run to. There seems to be a yearning in my heart for that period. I'd like to live each of those days in good health. Everything was so . . . meticulous then."

Within the strict confines his psyche imposed, Crazy Herbie was creating a fantasy cosmos for himself, rich with emotion. It is that vision—not its accoutrements—that makes him a celebrity today. One generation's outcast is another's superstar.

No one calls him Crazy Herbie anymore. He lives in ornamental splendor now, brushing up against the haute monde and signing autographs for the maid. His suite at Caesar's Palace is brimming over with gold leaf and crushed velvet. And from the window of his living room, you can see that billboard, with just the word TINY peering over the horizon.

He rises late, to a breakfast of honey and sunflower seeds. This is the basis of his celebrated diet—although he wavers from it in expansive moods. On his first night in Vegas, he ordered everything on the room-service menu. The bill came to $185, and when the food arrived, Tiny arranged it all over his suite and then just sat in the middle of it. Word raced through the hotel that he had actually rolled in all that food, but this he emphatically denies. "I saw it in an Edward Arnold movie," he explains.

• • •

I arrive at his suite at 4:00 p.m. Tiny's production manager, Ron De Blasio, ushers me into a plush chair and fetches me a Diet-Rite. De Blasio is largely responsible for the "class" drapes, dry-ice fog, and pirouetting chorines in togas. (They call it "the Botticelli number.") There are no Tiny Tim dolls on the market yet, but De Blasio admits he was tempted by an offer from a ukulele company. "We turned it down," he explains, "because we figured that in six weeks, every kid in the country would have one. Then Tiny would get known as a novelty."

That seems to be the strategy behind this promotion campaign. They are selling Tiny like a presidential candidate who must last awhile. After all, his talent runs deeper than his drag. The voices he sings in range from baritone to soprano. His practiced ear can absorb almost any vocal style, and his current act includes some flawless blasts from the distant past (Rudy Vallee, Russ Columbo, Cab Calloway—even Elvis Presley). His managers are letting the public experience Tiny an octave at a time.

"Hell—o, Mr. Goldstein." Tiny greets me with bouquets of daffodils in his voice. But I remain suspicious. Deep down, I want to discover the real (i.e., decadent) Tiny Tim. I want to write about the plastic cruelty of his public, or the poison suckle of his managers. But my slant has already been undermined by his fans—especially the kids. They sneak up to the front desk and ask to speak with Tiny on the house phone. They run down the corridors giggling at the mention of his name. Occasionally, they knock on my door, convinced I'm a distant cousin possessing some contagious magic. I ask a transfixed 4-year-old why Tiny Tim is so special. "Because he's all cute," she stammers, then runs off giggling.

Tiny himself is mystified by the marshmallow glee he inspires. He is confident that the children will tire of him, as they did of Soupy Sales. But his appeal among the very young may be more durable than he thinks. He has never cultivated kids, yet they seek him out at every concert. In fact, Tiny Tim is the only recent children's celebrity to emerge without benefit of regular exposure on daytime television.

To understand why, it's necessary to consider what a clown accomplishes, because children experience clowns differently than the rest of us do. They know that slapstick is a ruse to disarm an audience. Once we are in that state, a clown can move us with the mere suggestion of emotion or the flick of a prop. Great clowns balance fear, pity, mischief, and ridicule on the tips of their noses.

And the truly immortal clown—a harlequin for the ages—balances the most slippery emotion of all: innocence. He can make us feel holy by putting us in the company of one who has never sinned.

● ● ●

Far from the ebb and flow of slot machines, Tiny slips a pair of earphones over his antelope's head and smears his neck with Vicks VapoRub. Warms the throat.

"This one is short and sweet," booms the control room.

"Yes, Mr. Perry." Everyone is Mister or Miss to Tiny. If he doesn't know your last name he is liable to call you something like Mister Richard.

"Take a look at those words." Tiny picks up the envelope at his side and studies the lyrics he's supposed to cut today. It's "Hello, Hello," the Sopwith Camel hit, filled with self conscious innocence. Maybe a little too self-conscious for Tiny. He says, "It needs more words, it's too new. Can I change it around?"

De Blasio rushes in. "It's so you, Tiny. . . . It fits you like a suit. . . . Don't you see? . . . This makes great *sense* to sing."

That last phrase hits Tiny right between the eyes. When they mess with his music, Tiny starts to growl ("UMMMFFFF") and if they persist, he breaks into an intolerable whine. But words like "sense" are powerful tranquilizers, and they can be dangled above his head like a pacifier.

The song is cut in twenty takes. Tiny's voice is nearly gone, and his throat reeks of Vicks. But when the session breaks, he finds a piano at the back of the studio and begins to play. "A hit can be made in the bathtub," he observes as I pull up an extra chair. "You don't need these big studios. But everything's so technical today."

We talk about his music. He throws a dozen names at me from the antique charm bracelet in his mind. Names like Henry Burr and Billy Murray, Irving Kauffman, Anita Jones. "I'd like to use more of their authentic sounds in my music. I want to try singing through a megaphone to give people a sense of what actually went on."

Then he begins to play a song I've never heard before. Its melody is pure music box, and his voice is the toy ballerina spinning on top.

If I could drive a spaceship
I'd take you to the stars
And you would be alone with me
As we fly next to Venus and Mars . . .

As he sings, I feel a smile spreading across my face. His voice is so gentle, so powerful, and so sad. Tiny looks up, and I can see him blush.

De Blasio rushes in from the control booth. "We'll put it in the show tonight. It's beautiful, Tiny. Doncha see? It's about this guy who would do anything for his chick — even go to the moon. But he just hasn't got the stuff. He's so beautiful, though, because he's up there on the moon already, so he doesn't care."

Tiny winces and begins to grunt. "I don't do my own numbers in public," he says flatly. "Because these songs are written especially for girls. I wrote that for Miss Snookie, at the Page Three."

De Blasio studies the perforations in the soundproof ceiling. "But Tiny," he whispers, "that just doesn't make sense."

For two years Tiny sang at the Page Three, a Greenwich Village club "where the ladies liked each other." He insists that engagement was more meaningful than his current supergig at Caesar's Palace. In 1963, that cellar was the nexus of his existence, the one place where his outer and inner worlds met and made music together.

When he came on, all fidgeting ceased, and the ladies settled back into their seats. Then the lights went up on this scrawny mantis plucking a uke and bouncing on the balls of his feet. And then he sang:

If you ever said good bye
I'd feel depressed and yet
I'd never cry
For you would always be

27

In every memory
You are heaven here on
earth to me.

After his act was over, they stomped and shrieked for more. And the gargoyle onstage—who went to all of their parties and spent his spare bread cutting records for the ladies he loved—would blow these whispy puffs of gratitude from his lips.

What moved them then—and still does—is an aura of innocence so potent that it transcends Tiny's surroundings and makes him seem holy. I ask him to define purity, and he surprises me by answering with the ease of a man who is aware of his effect on others. "It's a spiritual fulfillment which comes with obeying God's laws."

The apostate in me bristles. I draw angry boxes around his words on my pad. "Which are God's laws?"

"Well, the first test is with women. We're not supposed to touch women until marriage. That means, no kissing or contact—except for talking."

"But what if your body tells you it's right to kiss a woman?"

"There are devil's angels and heaven's angels. A devil's angel will say it's perfectly permissible. But then, he couldn't be an angel from heaven because that kind of angel would follow heaven's laws."

"What happens if you disobey these laws?" I ask.

His voice drops to a firm baritone. "Ah—you suffer."

It would be a mistake to label Tiny Tim a puritan. He is too tolerant of sin in others and would probably make a lousy inquisitor. ("People's scenes don't bother me," he explains, "because I'm not after anything.") But his managers are aware of his worldview, and don't think they aren't prepared to exploit it. Says De Blasio: "I've often thought, looking at that profile, that some day I'd like Tiny to do a record of Bible readings."

"Even when I was younger, my father said I looked like Jesus," he admits.

"How did it feel being told that?"

"Very tempestuous. It frightened me to look like Christ."

Tiny is the product of a mixed marriage (father, Jewish; mother, Catholic). That he favors his dear mother should

28

be no surprise, since his cosmology is centered on women. He shuns all male toiletries and keeps a generous supply of cosmetic creams. ("This new cream—I ordered 150 jars—it makes your face look just like a julep.") Yet, those who are consoled by the notion that Tiny is a transvestite (or at least gay) are in for a rude shock. He is as straight as a yardstick and just as flexible. He is convinced that S-E-X (he won't even utter the word, or any other "swear," except for a plaintive "sh—ucks") is evil unless sanctioned by marriage, and he can't get married unless he sees a sign from heaven.

"Maybe in the next world, I'll have all the women I want," he muses, "but not in this one."

"Do you . . . want to sleep with women?"

"Yesss." He nearly falls off his seat with eagerness. "I don't want to behave this way. But it's one of God's supreme laws, you see. It's like going against a red light. Oh, it's so hard sometimes. I try never to be alone with a beautiful woman. Because, when I'm alone, the devil in me becomes dangerous."

"What happens then?"

"Well . . . ," he slides into his deepest voice yet. "I have fallen a few times." I blink and take a hefty swig of Diet-Rite. "But if I do something with a girl, I can't see her again unless it's like nothing ever happened. I've got to cut the cancer out and start anew."

I am unprepared to deal with Tiny Tim as a functioning heterosexual, so I begin to nibble on the end of my pen, a sure sign that I've lost control of the interview.

"I got involved with someone in 1966," he continues. "I had never gone with a woman before, but I said yes to her. I found out I'm no good to be tied down. She tried to have me stop my cosmetics. There was bickering night and day."

"Why do you wear makeup?"

"Oh, when I put on my face, I feel that I'm in a garden of paradise alone with beautiful ladies. They are the essence of my soul, a purity that cannot be tainted."

Dinner has arrived. A beaming waiter wheels in eight goblets of sherbet and two huge malteds. For the voice. I make motions to leave, but first I ask Tiny what he would do if he ever met his soul mate for real. He stops and gazes out at the gold lamé sunset in the distance. "I'll do anything to get her into my web," he says. "I've go to know her . . . to keep her. If nothing else works . . . I'll get to her boyfriend."

With fifteen minutes until show time, we sit in Tiny's dressing room talking about Johnny Carson ("I feel nothing but gratitude toward him") and Bob Dylan ("He believed in me from the very start") and John Lennon ("He was supposed to introduce me at the Albert Hall, but now I believe it's going to be Prince Philip. Can you imagine what Princess Margaret's face creams must be like?").

I have to confront him with a final myth: the one that claims success is killing Tiny Tim. He doesn't look moribund to me, but there are persistent reports of orgies and all-night drunks. His manager did have to move in with him at one point, and De Blasio still shares his quarters occasionally. So I pop the question, fully expecting a sanctimonious denial. Instead, he replies for real.

"When I first came to Hollywood, there were lots of temptations. It was so new, so strange . . . like going to the top of a mountain that so many try to climb. After you get there, you linger awhile and rest. I did have a drink here and there, though I didn't like the bitter taste. You know, back in May, I was alone in a hotel room. So I had a few. And I had a few people over. And I spent some money. I was dizzy . . . I've been that way before."

Maybe what the underground can't accept is Tiny's willing embrace of success. Show business is such a squid, why would anyone hustle it willingly? But Herberto Buckingham Kaury has always wanted to make it big, and that has always meant Las Vegas and candy fog and dancing girls. He would even sacrifice his innocence if it made *sense*. He is aware of alternatives, and strong enough to choose. His choice for now is that it is better to burn in neon than to freeze in the dark. Tiny remembers the dark well. He used to deliver dentures in it, when that was the only work he could get.

"I fought for this challenge all along," he says. "It's like a ball game for me. Every show is another inning."

So I leave him with his manager and climb a long flight of stairs until I can see the entire backstage of that velvet veldt they call the Circus Maximus. Vestal virgins grab a smoke in the wings, and, amid the tangle of cardboard columns, orchestral clatter fills the air. Tiny Tim is also warming up. I see him in a corner, trotting in place and flaying the air with his hands. Then he goes into his windup: right hand back, left foot out, and there's the pitch—a wicked spitball curve. And he watches, delighted, as the batter in his head strikes out.

—1968

CHAPTER 5

The Lizard King

LOS ANGELES—"The shaman . . . he was a man who would intoxicate himself. See, he was probably already an . . . uh . . . unusual individual. And, he would put himself into a trance by dancing, whirling around, drinking, taking drugs—however. Then, he would go on a mental travel and . . . uh . . . describe his journey to the rest of the tribe."
—JIM MORRISON

He comes to meet you in superstar fatigues: a slept-in pull-over and the inevitable leather pants. A lumpy hat covers most of his mane. You mutter "groovy" at each other in greeting, and split for the beach. His most recent song comes on the radio. You both laugh as he turns up the volume and fiddles with the bass controls. It's a perfect afternoon, so he picks up his girl. She says, "Your hat makes you look like a Rembrandt, Jim," and he whispers, "Oh, wow."

Between freeways, you talk about his bust in New Haven (the charge: indecent and immoral exhibition), Vietnam, psychoanalysis, and his new album. He wants to call it *The Celebration of the Lizard* after a 24-minute "drama" he has just composed. He is into reptiles. He wants the album's jacket printed in pseudo-snakeskin, with its title embossed in gold.

The official interview takes place in a sequestered inlet at the Garden of Self-Realization, an ashram Hollywood style. You sit not far from an úrn certified to contain Mahatma Gandhi's ashes. Music is piped in from speakers at the top of a stucco arch with cupolas sprayed gold. The ground on which you are assembling your tape recorder is filled with worms. They seem to be surfacing around his hands, and he examines one as you set the mike in place. Amid a burst of strings from the hidden

33

speakers, you ask a trial question: "When you started, did you anticipate your image?"

Jim answers in a slithering baritone: "Nahhh. It just sort of happened . . . unconsciously."

"How did you prepare yourself for stardom?"

"Uh . . . about the only thing I did was . . . I stopped getting haircuts."

"How has you behavior onstage changed?"

"See, it used to be . . . I'd just stand still and sing. Now, I . . . uh . . . exaggerate a little bit."

He gives a cautious, mischievous interview, contemplating each question as though it were a hangnail, and answering with just a trace of smile in the quotation marks: "I'm beginning to think it's easier to scare people than to make them laugh."

"I wonder why people like to believe I'm high all the time. I guess maybe they think someone else can take their trip for them."

"A game is a closed field . . . a ring of death with . . . uh . . . sex at the center. Performing is the only game I've got, so . . . I guess it's my life."

His statements, like his songs, are unpunctuated puzzles. You connect the dots between images, and become involved. "I'm a word man," he exults. "See, there's this theory about the nature of tragedy, that Aristotle didn't mean catharsis for the audience, but a purgation of emotions for the actors themselves. The audience is just a witness to the event taking place onstage."

He suggests you read Nietzsche on the nature of tragedy to understand where he is really at. His eyes glow as he launches into a discussion of the Apollonian-Dionysian struggle for control of the life force. No need to guess which side he's on.

"See, singing has all the things I like," he explains. "It's involved with writing and with music. There's a lot of acting. And it has this one other thing . . . a physical element . . . a sense of the immediate. When I sing, I create characters."

"What kinds of characters?"

"Oh . . . hundreds. Hundreds of 'em."

"I like to think he just arrived—
you know, came out of nowhere"

—A FAN

He was born James Douglas Morrison, under the sign of Sagittarius, the hunter, in Melbourne, Florida, 24 years ago. He once told a reporter, "You could say I was ideally suited for the work I'm doing. It's the feeling of a bow string being pulled back for 22 years and suddenly let go."

But he won't discuss those years on the taut end of existence. He would like you to accept his appearance as a case of spontaneous generation—America's love-lion spurting full grown from the neon loins of the sixties. "They claim everyone was born, but I don't remember it," he insists. "Maybe I was having one of my blackouts."

To accept the thumbnail sketch he offers, there is little in Jim's past to account for his presence. His father is an admiral, but he doesn't think that explains his fascination with authority. His family moved so often that his most immediate childhood memories are of landscapes, but that suggests nothing to him about his current shiftlessness. (He lives in motels, or with friends.)

Jim parries questions about his personal experience with acrobatic agility. You find yourself wondering whether he can manipulate his image with the same consummate ease. Does his dark side appear at random, or can he summon the lunatic within the way most of us put on a telephone voice? You keep trying to catch him in a moment of prefabricated magic, but any attempt to grasp Jim Morrison is repelled by that fortress of ego, which is yet another of his personae. Behind the walls, however, you sense a soft, slippery kid, who was probably lonely and certainly bored.

"I was a good student. Read a lot. But I was always . . . uh . . . talking when I wasn't supposed to. They made me sit at a special table . . . nothing bad enough to get kicked out, of course. I got through school. . . . Went to Florida State University . . . mainly because . . . I couldn't think of anything else to do."

He came west after college to attend the UCLA film school. He lived alone in Venice, among the muddy canals and peeling colonnades. The roof of a deserted warehouse was his office. He spent most of his free time there, writing and making his way through the literary underground. He was brooding (now they say "intense") and shy (in the fan magazines, "sensitive").

A classmate recalls: "He was a lot like he is now, but nobody paid much attention then."

At UCLA, Morrison met Ray Manzarek, a young filmmaker and jazz pianist on the side. For a while they shared a tiny flat, and Jim began to share his poems as well. It was Manzarek who thought of setting them to music. And though he had never sung before, Jim spent the next few months exploring his voice. Drummer John Densmore and guitarist Robbie Krieger added sturdy hinges to the sound of the Doors. With Manzarek skimming the keyboard of an electric organ, the new group was tight and sinewy from the start. They did bread gigs at small clubs along the Sunset Strip, reworking rock-blues standards and staking out a milieu. But they spent most of their dormant period implementing the controlled insanity that Jim Morrison was to loose on rock.

"We all play a lead and subjugation things with each other," explains Ray. "When Jim gets into something, I'm able to give of that area within myself. We may look cool, but we are really evil, insidious cats behind Jim. We instigate the violence in him. A lot of times he doesn't feel particularly angry but the music just drives him to it."

This total immersion of sentiment in sound amplifies Morrison's lyrics, transforming them into something more like pageant than poetry. Onstage, his voice becomes a fierce rattle, and his rap a spell. In a tiny sweat-cellar, or a stadium, or on the radio in stereophonic sound: magic. They put a spell on you.

"Think of us as erotic politicians."

—Jim Morrison to *Newsweek*

Elvis Presley's hillbilly grace is now a patriarchal paunch. But none of the rock titans who followed him has inherited his crown. Even the Beatles built their empire on clean energy ("Yeah, yeah, yeah") and later refined that base through the safe profundity of artsong. The Rolling Stones came close. Their message was the potency of sex, but the Stones were after rape, not soul plunder.

The Doors, however, are an inner theater of cruelty. Their musical dramas have made fear and trembling part of the rock lexicon. These days every band has a local lunatic singing lead.

But the Doors have already transcended their own image. Now they are in search of total sensual contact with an audience. They may yet appear at a future concert in masks. As Ray Manzarek explains: "We want our music to short-circuit the conscious mind and allow the subconscious to flow free."

That goal is a realization of what was implicit in Elvis Presley's sacred wiggle. But if Elvis was an unquestioning participant in his own hysteria, the Doors celebrate their myth as a deliberate creation. Playing sorcerer is Jim's thing—not a job, or a hobby, or even one of those rituals we sanctify with the name Role. "Play is not the same thing as a game," he explains. "A game involves rules. But play is an open event. It's free. Like, you know how people walk to where they're going—very orderly, right? But little kids . . . they're like dogs. They run around, touch things, sing a song. Well, actors play like that. Also, musicians. And you dig watching somebody play, because that's the way human beings are supposed to be . . . free. Like animals."

Words are Jim's playpen. He jots stanzas, images, and allusions into a leather-bound notebook, as they occur to him. These are shaped and sifted into the thought-collages that are the Doors' finished lyrics.

. . . Awkward instant
And the first animal is jettisoned,
Legs furiously pumping
Their stiff green gallop,
and heads bob up
Poise
Delicate
Pause
Consent
In mute nostril agony . . .

"See, this song is called 'Horse Latitudes' because it's about the Doldrums, where sailing ships from Spain would get stuck. In order to lighten the vessel, they had to throw things overboard. Their major cargo was working horses for the New World. And this song is about that moment when the horse is in air. I imagine it must have been hard to get them over the side. When they got to the edge, they probably starting chucking and kicking. And it must have been hell for the men to watch, too. Because horses can swim for a while, but then they lose their strength and just go down. . . slowly sink away."

Violence is his major motif. It permeates his music. His central symbol, the Great Snake, appears throughout the repertory of the Doors. Sometimes it is a phallic liberator, extolling an act of creative desecration. Sometimes it is a handy fetish to wave in the breeze, instead of the real thing. But most often, it is the agent of self-knowledge, residing in our imaginations and slinking toward consciousness to be born. Most Doors songs plead with us to reject all repressive authority and embrace the Great Snake, with its slippery equation of freedom and violence. It is an equation easier to execute in art than in life.

"Robbie and I were sittin' on a plane an' like it's first class, so you get a couple o' drinks, an' I said to Robbie, 'Y'know, there are the Apollonian people . . . like, very formal, rational dreamers. An' then there's the Dionysian thing . . . the insanity trip . . . way inside.' An' I said, 'You're an Apollonian . . . up there with your guitar . . . all neat an' thought out . . . y'know . . . an' you should get into the Dionysian thing.'

"An' he looks up at me an' says, 'Oh, yeah, right Jim.'"

The Lizard King slithers down Sunset Strip in a genuine snakeskin jacket and leather tights. Bands of teenyboppers flutter about, but he is oblivious. He moves past ticky-tacoramas and used-head shops into the open arms of recording studio B, where his true subjects wait.

He greets us with a grin out of "Thus Spake Zarathustra," and we realize instantly that Jim is loaded. Juiced. Stoned—the old way. Booze. No one is surprised; Jim is black Irish to the breath. He deposits a half-empty quart bottle of wine on top of the control panel and downs the remnants of somebody's beer.

"Hafta break it in," he mutters, caressing the sleeves of his jacket. It sits green and scaly on his shoulders, and crinkles like tinfoil whenever he moves.

"It's—very Tennessee Williams, Jim."

Grunt. He turns to producer Paul Rothchild with a spacious grin that says, "I'm here, so you can start," but Rothchild makes little clicking noises with his tongue. He is absorbed in a musical problem, and he offers only a perfunctory nod to the tipsy titan at his side.

Behind a glass partition, three musical Doors hunch over their instruments, intent on a rhythm line that refuses to render itself whole. The gap between Morrison and the other Doors is vast in the studio, where the enforced cohesion of live performance is missing. On their own, they are methodic musicians. Densmore drums in sharp, precise strokes. Krieger's guitar is sinuous but sober. And at the organ, Manzarek is cultivated and crisp. With his shaggy head atop a pair of plywood shoulders, he looks like a hip undertaker.

Jim walks into the studio and accosts a vacant mike. He writhes in languid agony, jubilant at the excuse to move in his new jacket. But Rothchild keeps the vocal mike dead, to assure maximum concentration on the problem at hand. From behind the glass partition, Jim looks like a silent movie of himself, speeded up for laughs. The musicians barely notice. When he is drinking, they work around him. Only Ray is solicitous enough to smile. The others tolerate him, as a pungent but necessary prop.

"I'm the square of the Western hemisphere," he says, returning to his wine. "Man . . . whenever somebody'd say something groovy . . . it'd blow my mind. Now, I'm learnin' . . . You like people? I hate 'em . . . screw 'em . . . I don't need 'em . . . Oh, I need 'em . . . to grow potatoes."

He teeters about the tiny room, digging his boots into the carpeting. Between belches, he gazes at each of us, smirking. But the seance is interrupted when Rothchild summons him. While Jim squats behind the control panel, a roughly recorded dub of his "Celebration of the Lizard" comes over the loudspeakers.

Gently, almost apologetically, Ray tells him the thing doesn't work. Too diffuse, too mangy. Jim's face sinks beneath his scaly collar. Right then, you can sense that "The Celebration of the Lizard" will never appear on record—certainly not on the new Doors album. There will be eleven driving songs, and snatches of poetry. But no Lizard King. No monarch crowned with love beads and holding the phallic scepter in his hand.

"Hey, bring your notebook to my house tomorrow morning, okay?" Rothchild offers.

"Yeah." Jim answers with the look of a dog who's just been told he's missed his walk. "Sure."

Defeated, the Lizard King seeks refuge within his scales. He disappears for ten minutes and returns with a bottle of brandy. Fortified, he closets himself inside an anteroom used to record isolated vocals. He turns the lights out, fits himself with earphones, and begins to play.

Crescendos of breath between the syllables. His song is half threat, and half plea:

Five to one baby
One in five
Nobody here
Gets out alive

Everyone in the room tries to bury Jim's presence in conversation. But his voice intrudes, bigger and blacker than life over the loudspeakers. Each trace of sound is magnified, so we can hear him guzzling and belching away. Suddenly, he emerges from his formica cell, inflicting his back upon a wall. He is sweat-drunk but still coherent, and he mutters so everyone can hear: "If I had an axe . . . man, I'd kill everybody . . . 'cept . . . uh . . . my friends."

Sagittarius the hunter stalks us with his glance. We sit frozen, waiting for him to spring.

"Ah—I hafta get one o' them Mexican wedding shirts," he sighs.

Robbie's girl, Donna, takes him on: "I don't know if they come in your size."

"I'm a medium . . . with a large neck."

"We'll have to get you measured, then."

"Uh-uh . . . I don't like to be measured." His eyes glow with sleep and swagger.

"Oh Jim, we're not gonna measure all of you. Just your shoulders."

—1968

40

CHAPTER 6
More Mysterioso

NEW YORK—John Kramer—songwriter, market researcher, musician, salesman of men's socks, folk singer, former owner of a Chicago mutt named Micky, current owner of a New York poodle named Dildo, and superstar-to-be—is 15 minutes late. He was due to begin an overdubbing session on his first record at 11 p.m. His label is Columbia, the most powerful in the world. After three years in New York at odd jobs and unemployment ("I'm selective about jobs; I select which days I want to work"), Sunbeam Music signed him. Now it pays $150 a month for John to sit home and write songs. Some titles: "Hello Roach," "God Don't Like Uglies," "Gonna Send You Back to Hackensack." The genre is difficult to describe.

John Kramer has always been nervous about recording. Pills don't help. They don't prevent the hoarseness and sore throat that always seem to attack him when he is about to sing. Cough medicine doesn't do any good. The cracking voice is a sure sign that John is due to record, as are headaches, insomnia, intense craving for Pepsi, and any number of other symptoms. Everyone kids about getting the "big break," but when it comes, everything is dead serious. John Kramer wants, more than anything else in this world, to be a big star. Columbia Records can make him that. So Columbia makes him nervous.

We meet at the recording studio, a converted church on the East Side. John is dressed in a cream-colored summer suit. A smile; a friendly interview-type handshake. He rings the night bell. No answer. He runs around the corner to call in, but the telephone is broken, so he loses his last dime. Back at the church, he slams at the bell and begs it to answer. Thirty minutes late, and only an echo. No one home. Shit.

"Hop into a cab. It's in the building on 52nd and Sixth."

John Kramer slumps into his seat, then jumps erect with a glance at his watch — 11:45 p.m. "They'll blame me; I know they will! Everybody knows where these things are but me. Columbia owns the whole city."

Three hangnails come off in John's mouth and are quickly digested. The taxi cruises leisurely past 42nd Street.

"They want me to change my name," John reports. "John Oliver—the Crispian-Saint-French-Fry kind of thing."

We stop for a light.

"How does Arthur Nouveau hit you?" John asks.

"How about Seashell and Carbuncle?" I inquire. But the cab has stopped and John bounds ahead. We march through the immense black demi-columns and into the controlled climate of an office building. We race into an elevator in a frantic search for Recording Studio A. We careen past rows of offices and reception desks. Each department looks like an airport waiting room: pop and op adorn the walls. We enter Studio A, facing a hostile row of screens and three very grim-looking men. We have wandered by mistake into Studio A-WCBS Radio, and are summarily thrown out. Out into the hot street for a trot over to Broadway, where still another Columbia edifice stands. John says, "My throat feels like a furnace."

Columbia recording studio. Enter John Kramer—one hour late, despite frequent warnings from his agent about being on time. Still muttering, "They're going to blame me," he rings for the elevator. A porter reveals that it's locked. We race around the block and enter through an alley that smells of chop suey. Up four flights of sweating stairs and into a door marked, at last, Studio A.

At 12, John Kramer played cymbals for the American Legion Marching Drum and Bugle Corps. At 12 1/2, he broke his nose between two smashing cymbals—always the enthusiast where music is concerned.

John's parents and grandmother still live in an old house on Chicago's Near North side. The gas furnace in their living room explodes into action every so often, covering the walls with a blue flame glow and emitting a sound of roasting popcorn. Hillbillies live upstairs.

Today John lives in a small studio in Brooklyn Heights. His instruments, his stuffed owl named Louise, and his collage of Jean Harlow and Ringo adorn the walls.

John's A&R man at Columbia is Howard Roberts. He is tops in his field, and he approaches every session with the assurance of a man who has seen the word "star" written on many hands and faces. Three men are present with Howard in the studio. One will control the flow of prerecorded music over which John sings. One will work the decibel knobs. And one, a friend, will certify the soulfulness.

"John, you're late."

John Kramer sits alone in the recording studio. They have turned out the lights and placed him behind an immense acoustical screen. Instruments are scattered around the room. The ceiling is covered with a thick, soundproof coat.

John takes off his tie and shoes, loosens his belt, and gulps water. Every nervous swallow is audible in the control booth. John is recording his first single, an up-tempo number called "The Moving Finger Writes." Columbia has added a Gypsy-flavored background to John's lyrics, so that the sound is in the "Sonny and Cher bag."

For the first three takes, John's voice is hoarse and hesitant. Howard cuts in. "This is your first statement to the world and it has to be strong and dramatic. These are your words—it's your sound. I don't care how much ham you have to use. Let the world know you're here and now. Let them know you count."

Howard's peptalk registers. By take number eight, John's voice is strong. His newfound power shakes the control booth. By the tenth take, they are down to minor points. "Get a little cry into that phrase," says Howard.

"They expect soul from me?" John asks. "I'm from the Midwest." It is 1:00 a.m., so nobody laughs. Minor flubs on the next two takes bring the total to fifteen. Howard announces, "This will be it, John."

The music begins. There is Chicago, and those forgotten engagements with three clean-cut folk musicians who toured the region as part of a hootenanny package and did commercials for Orange Crush. There is New York City—mooched meals, a room at the YMCA, living with friends in the Bronx, and borrowing movie money. Promises from another record company don't pan out, and all those smiling faces ask "But what do you *do*, John?"

What he does is entertain. Now, there is nothing left to do but sing. In that soundproof cavern is everything that John Kramer has ever wanted. In those black control knobs are all the status any pop idol can handle. John pats the microphone tenderly. Inside are the current and velocity to make him a star. A big, BIG star.

The moving finger writes
And having written moves away
And nothing we can say or do
Can make a change
No tears can wash these words away . . .

Take fifteen is over. Howard's friend is still mouthing lyrics. The man at the knobs lights his eighth cigarette. John is chewing on the remnant of his last whole fingernail.

A critic's silence. Howard opens his eyes and whispers, groans, implores, "More mysterioso."

Back into the booth for another try. If John Kramer makes it, he will be able to hire fingernails to bite on. But at 3:00 a.m., he is out of cuticles.

"Cue me, Howard."

Six months after he staggered home from that session, John Kramer awoke from a night of troubled dreams—at 2:00 p.m. He put his phone back on the hook, and stumbled out of bed. A deflated tube of toothpaste lay like a starved rat across his bathroom sink. The soap was gathering dust.

No one had phoned all morning. All last month he had waited to be awakened by news of an agent's bonus, a hot flash from the record company, a long-distance love letter from some fan in Phoenix or Terre Haute. But the phone was haughty in its silence, so John kept it off the hook mornings—so he could sleep.

A rotting avocado yawned at him from the refrigerator. He swilled the flattened remnants of last night's Pepsi and thought about making tea. Or buying milk. Or going out to eat. Nothing you can do with a rotten avocado.

John was flat broke. Spare change gone, he had taken to crawling under the bed, flashlight in hand, to search out dimes and quarters. No more pop bottles to change for laundry money. Twice last week, John had thought of calling Western Union to send himself a candygram—the vague reality of eventual payment seemed puny next to the immediacy of lunch.

And so today. Radio brings The Word: Sam the Sham does his shtick with the Shamettes. John Kramer hates that song more than he hates the kid who used to beat him up when he was 8. More than he hates the super who left the heat off, freezing John's parakeet Rosalie. More than the friend who accompanied him to that session six months ago, and hasn't said a thing about it since, although, as a rock critic, he could put a word in where it counts. ("Problems," the friend had moaned in their last conversation. "The phone rings from nine till five, continually; it never stops.")

Today they are releasing John Kramer's follow-up record. Follow-up to what, you ask? John straightens to all of his wheat-jeaned sixfootness and answers: "The Moving Finger Writes"—a willowy ballad written during a literary lull. Columbia chose it as John's debut single. As the song took shape, it grew distant. After sixteen takes in a recording studio, it was as glitzy as a two-cents plain. They substituted an orchestra oozing minor notes for John's acoustic accompaniment. They stretched John's curt midwestern vocal into a parody of swirling sobbing vibrato—something they call, "mysterioso." In the tedious process, the haunting sparseness of John's lyric, its delicate blend of whimsy and mockery, became bold and brazen. In other words, overkill.

Something slippery was wrong. And John never did speak up, though it must have crossed his icy fingertips that morning to blurt out: "I am not Tony Bennett in ethnic drag. I am not Bluesbelly, that obscure bayou singer newly rediscovered. I am John Kramer from the Near North side of Chicago, and I am about as mysterioso as a plate of squash."

John downed his second cup of weak tea from yesterday's tea bag. He put on the Levi's he had spent hours bleaching in the sun and the sneakers he had gnawed into misshape. Outside, it was a leafy Brooklyn Heights afternoon. Where does one go to mark the release date of one's follow-up single? What do they do with all the unsold copies? John imagined a warehouse of failure located somewhere on the fringe of Tin Pan Alley. Floor upon floor of unwanted ego. Dust clogs the grooves until they vanish. And the whole room reeks of new record smell.

The final irony—yes, of course—the new Len Barry release is something called "The Moving Finger Writes." Something very different from John's songs, and titles can't be copyrighted. Something infinitely more . . . mysterioso.

—1966

CHAPTER 7

Mover

NEW YORK—Even over the phone, he kisses, then slaps, you with his voice. Hit-and-run chatter bristles across the wires. He'll call again tomorrow, twice, to bawl you out for staying away from his club last night, when it was all absolutely happening, positively, man.

Last year, Steve Paul owned Manhattan's most envied discotheque, the Scene. His club sprawled over the cellar of a West Side building like the amorphous arms of some massive sewage system. The place was full of corners; you could always find privacy in all that public.

The Scene was its own attraction. Nightly, to a wall-to-wall audience, it acknowledged applause from hands limp with reputation. It accepted ebullient nods from celebrities and praise from show-biz extras who spent their unwinding hours on the dance floor. The brush-up-against effect was electric. It grew known, renowned, and In.

Steve Paul got his picture in a lot of papers. *Newsweek* chronicled "the sad demise of the Stork Club and the explosive emergence of the Scene" in one week. The *New York Times* contributed five columns of newsprint and three photo layouts. Society columnists made the club their salon-of-the-moment; Tennessee Williams met his understudies over frug and frenzy. Sammy Davis, Jr., sang for free. The Great Discovery happened: another plebeian palace ready to be plucked by the withered, with-it overworld. His club was the real thing—a controlled slum, the kind that doesn't knife you if you walk through at 4:00 a.m. So everyman who was anybody showed up to sit in a corner. And Steve Paul poured on the sauce.

47

"The Scene was THE club in New York in the true sense and the business sense and the hip sense and the decency sense."

"We aimed at happenings in a nonstructured way. Nothing happened, but things occurred from time to time."

"There was no differentiation in terms of structure between audience, staff, and entertainers."

"There was a certain honesty and decency and creativity, so naturally it was special."

"It was a tremendously secure world of nightly occurrence. Everybody was like turned-on and jumping around with the club, and I would like to go into the back room and cry."

Steve Paul is one light-year older now. His reputation lies strewn across a couch, a cornucopia yellowing at the corners.

In a *Journal-American* article calling him the "folk-rock philosopher," he admits "Of course, sex plays an important part in discotheque dancing." He displays two columns by Dick Schaap, side by side. One is a put-up, one a put-down. He loves both. Someone calls his club a "murky, mad cellar." He chuckles over "my hippest piece of publicity," an article by Pete Hamill that accuses him of being "part of the lie that it is more important to be hip than good."

"You're in the center, man, when you're mentioned in other people's columns," he says. "Truth and groove win out, right man?"

Steve Paul doesn't sing or dance or tell funny stories. He brings it all together. This is hard work with lousy hours. The only fringe benefit is fame. So Steve Paul stands in the door of his club drinking in the crowd, searching for FACES among the coats and hats. As emcee, he sometimes sits at the feet of his entertainers. No one has actually seen him cry onstage, but he claims he has for so long that everyone believes it. It's part of the cool.

"He's all wrapped up in ego like an onion."

"He uses lots of words, but he's still nonverbal."

"He's a mess who moves things."

He lives on the ragged edge of the Village in a townhouse. His block looks like the bottom of a chestnut vendor's barrel—with soot from warehouses, grease from all-night diners, and fog that creeps across the river and down the street. Inside is the Scene without spotlights. Each room is tastefully overdecorated. Walls of exposed brick are bathed in murky half-light. The refrigerator is covered with Contac.

"I refurbished this place by adding myself," your host offers, watching to see that written down. Making good copy is something he learned at 17, when he was a public relations man. Interviewing Steve Paul is like watching the dance of the seven veils. There is veil number one before you: Stevie-baby the PR man, churning out copy. "The Scene is part of the continuing search for me to express myself," he begins, waiting tastefully until the words can be recorded. "I have no throne and I feel sorry for my pretenders because it doesn't exist. I'm in competition with nobody."

His delivery of Paulisms—those epigrammatic gems that go nowhere but look great—is flawless. What do you want in an idol, Steve? "Myself plus one." In a girl? "Herself plus one." A friend? "An equal." If you let him, Steve Paul gives a write-it-yourself interview.

"I gave away two thousand button-paintings because of my feeling that art should be extended everywhere till people understand that art is life and life is art. No promotion, just for the groove of it." Veil number two: Steve the artiste, the stage-struck savant. "There are two realities: the world of universal reality (which is the ability to achieve what you want from the social machinery) and the world of personal reality (which is your emotions). To exist in one or the other is to exist in nothing. The only thing that matters is to be in the world of spiritual reality, which is synthesis."

Veil three: Steve the celebrity. A chance guest shot on the *Les Crane Show* brought him a flood of letters and a show of his own. "I was the hottest thing in America," he recalls. "All those columns, all that space—you're a journalist, do you realize what that means?"

Paul's first TV show turned out to be an autobiography looking for its subject. It was also his last. The publicity, too, came and went, and the Scene began to founder; then it sank.

49

Gross went down to one-third of peak. Paul refuses to blame the club's decline on the rise of nouveau-chic discos along Third Avenue, or the departure of those searchers after plebe-rock to a real slum on the Lower East Side. He says: "We were busy being busy instead of grooving. It was a matter of repeating spontaneity."

Steve Paul must have spent a few memorable nights in his townhouse during his downfall. But he never acknowledges depression. Veil number four has "I am an achiever-believer" written all over it. Decline is reconstruction. Steve Paul is renovating the Scene into a hip Disneyland, with a stellar cast from the avant-garde freaking freely over the same crags and crannies the celebs used to chic in. He has constructed an impressive lineup; the Blues Project, Muddy Waters, the Rascals, and Tim Hardin in his first New York engagement. Allen Ginsberg is slated to lead audiences in singing chants and mantras. Steve Paul is opening his club to a new kind of aristocracy, the plastic galaxy of the New Bohemia.

"If one person—ME—can turn on Bob Dylan and *Newsweek* in one week, and get Allen Ginsberg and Murray the K to donate their services, he would have to be, at the least, not a bad person, and a success," he reasons. The code of the mover: product is all. Currently, product is the Velvet Underground, belting spectral atonality while Andy Warhol programs an "underground amateur hour." A mod wedding with a guru officiating is in the offing, and Paul is thinking of holding onstage auditions for the lucky couple. The underground has already met Tin Pan Alley. At the Scene, it will touch Seventh Avenue. When you're cooking with chic, anything is possible, even friendship with Andy Warhol. "First we met to exploit each other," Paul explains. "Then for whatever we could do for each other. And then as people who appreciate the aspects of tragedy and absurdity of our times."

But Steve Paul's life is more like a William Burroughs truism: "Selling is more of a habit than using." Steve Paul Associates handled publicity for the Peppermint Lounge before its founder was old enough to drink there. Steve Paul speculated on the stock market as an adolescent. Steve Paul dropped out of Dobbs Ferry, took refuge from NYU and lived in everything from a room at the Y to a penthouse down the block. "Until I was 19 or 20, I was completely full of shit. I felt uncomfortable being full of shit," he says uncomfortably. "I was concerned with power for power's sake, and money for money's sake."

Now Steve Paul Associates handles one client. More veils slide off as he loses his cool. He switches masks on command, speeding on my lack of sympathy. You can see it in the corners of his eyes—my god, this guy is writing a piece on me, and he doesn't dig me—he really doesn't dig me. Steve Paul almost cries.

Veil five—the hippie put-down—slips off seductively. Veil six—at least I'm honest—wriggles free. And now it is down to underthings: Steve Paul the mixed-up kid. In his kitchen, he scrapes the walls of his ego in search of material—always new material.

"See, when I was a kid I used to lie and steal." He licks his lips. "I stole from my mother. See, there was this bureau; I still remember it. There was three drawers and the one on the right was verboten. I used to cop quarters and things. When I was older, I'd steal from my roommate, go out and spend $6 on food and say it cost 9, you owe me $4.50—a million things like that."

His eyes stop moving for the first time that evening. "I just stopped it . . . first the big lies and then the little ones . . . then everything. And now, what hangs me up man . . . wow . . . I tell the truth and still think I'm lying. I have to tell myself, hey stop telling that, and then I realize . . . man, it's all really happening."

There is a certain beauty in the pure act of hustling, in Steve Paul's dream of "meaning no evil but not being especially hung up on the good." But he will never appreciate his own aesthetic. Instead he walks a line between hustling and grooving. He tries, by his own definition, "to worm my way in without being wormy." He succeeds where it shows. He fills his empty house with phone calls. He marshals Andy Warhol's people together like a den mother ("Andy's at the Stalls? I mean, the Sculls? Well, get him over to the club; the *New York Post* wants to do a photo layout. C'mon, you've gotta move"). His chest expands over the phone, his legs cross languidly. On the radio, Murray the K is interviewing Tim Hardin. More good works. Steve Paul got these men together. An hour before, when Murray called, complaining that Hardin was late, Steve explained about artists and poetic license. When he listens to the interview actually happening, he beams, and shakes his head, and chuckles: "Wow."

Steve Paul feels real when he moves things.

—1966

CHAPTER 8

San Francisco Bray

SAN FRANCISCO—Forget the cable cars; skip Chinatown and the Golden Gate; don't bother about the topless mother of eight. San Francisco is the Liverpool of the West. *Newsweek* says so. *Ramparts* says so. And thousands of scenieboppers all over the nation wish they were here.

The most fragile thing to maintain in our culture is an underground. No sooner does a new tribe of rebels skip out, flip out, trip out, and take its stand, than photographers from *Life* magazine are on the scene doing a cover. No sooner is a low-rent, low-harassment quarter discovered than it appears in eight-color spreads on America's breakfast table. American culture is a store window that must be periodically spruced and dressed. The new bohemians needn't worry about opposition these days—just exploitation.

The new music from San Francisco, most of it unrecorded at this writing, is the most potentially vital in the pop world. It shoots a cleansing wave over the rigid studiousness of rock. It brings driving spontaneity to a music that is becoming increasingly conscious of form and influence rather than effect. Most important, if the sound succeeds, it will establish a new brand of culture hero with a new message: pop mysticism.

Talent scouts from a dozen major record companies are grooving with the gathered tribes at the Fillmore and the Avalon. Hip San Francisco is being carved into bits of business territory. The Jefferson Airplane belong to RCA. Sopwith Camel did so well for Kama Sutra the label has invested in a second local group, the Charlatans. The Grateful Dead have signed with Warner Brothers in an extraordinary deal that gives them complete control over material and production. Moby Grape is tinkering with Columbia and Electra. All because San Francisco is the Liverpool of the West.

Not many bread-men understand the electronic rumblings from beneath the Golden Gate, but they are aware of two crucial factors: the demise of Merseybeat created a doldrums that resulted in the rise of rhythm and blues and Milquetoast music, but left the white teenage audience swooning over an acknowledged fraud—the Monkees. Youth power still makes the pop industry move, and record executives know a fad sometimes needs no justification for success except its presence in a sympathetic time. There is the feeling now, as pop shepherds watch the stars over their grazing flock, that if the San Francisco sound isn't the next Messiah, it will at least give the profits a run for their money.

"The important thing about San Francisco rock 'n' roll," says Ralph Gleason, "is that the bands here all sing and play live, and not for recordings. You get a different sound at a dance. It's harder and more direct."

Gleason, influential jazz and pop music critic for the *San Francisco Chronicle*, writes with all the excitement of a participant. But he maintains the detachment of 20 years' experience. Gleason's thorough comprehension of the new sound is no small factor in its growth and acceptance by the city at large. He is a virtual tastemaker in San Francisco, and even when the hippies put him down, they talk to him and he listens.

That Gleason writes from San Francisco is no coincidence. This city's rapport with the source of its ferment is unique. Traveling up the coast from the ruins of the Sunset Strip to the Haight is a Dantesque ascent. Four hundred miles makes the difference between a neon wasteland and the most important underground in the nation. San Francisco has the vanguard because it works hard to keep it. Native culture is cherished as though the city's consuming passion were to produce a statement that could not possibly be duplicated in New York.

Ten years ago, San Franciscans frowned on North Beach, but let it happen. Now, the city is prepared to support the rock underground by ignoring it. The theory of tacit neglect means a de facto tolerance of psychedelic drugs. San Francisco is far and away the most turned-on city in the Western world. "The cops are aware of the number of heads here," says Bill Graham, who owns the Fillmore and manages the Jefferson Airplane. "The law thinks it will fade out, like North Beach. What can they do? To see a cop in the Haight . . . it's like the English invading China. Once they own it, how are they going to police it?"

The psychedelic ethic—still germinating and still unspoken—runs through the musical mainstream like a current. When Bob Weir of the Grateful Dead says, "The whole scene is like a contact high," he is not speaking in fanciful metaphor. Musical ideas are passed from group to group like a joint. There is an almost visible cohesion about San Francisco rock. With a scene that is small enough to navigate and big enough to make waves, with an establishment that all but provides the electric current, no wonder San Francisco is the Liverpool of the West.

"I didn't have any musical revelation when I took acid. I'm a musician first. My drug experiences are separate." The speaker is a member of the Jefferson Airplane, the oldest and most established group in the Bay Area. With a cohesive, vibrant sound, they are the hip community's first Product. Their initial album, *Jefferson Airplane Takes Off*, was weak enough to make you wonder about all the noise, but the new release, *Surrealistic Pillow*, is a fine collection of original songs with a tight and powerful delivery. The hit single, "My Best Friend," is a pleasant enough ballad, but much better is "White Rabbit," which is Alice in Wonderland with a twist of psychedelic lemon. Grace Slick's voice vibrates deliciously and the lyrics are concise and funny. Especially worth repeating is the song's advice: "Remember what the dormouse said: feed your head."

Turning on is an aspect of Bay Area rock, but it is by no means central to the music. The secretive reserve that characterizes every other hip community is unnecessary baggage here. There is open talk of drug experience. When references appear in the music, they are direct and specific. While some groups seem impaled on a psychedelic spear ("How do we talk about drugs without getting banned from the radio?" is a key question of every Byrds album), San Francisco music says "pot" and goes on to other things. Bob Weir of the Grateful Dead insists: "We're not singing psychedelic drugs, we're singing songs. We're musicians, not dope fiends."

He sits in the dining room of the three-story house he shares with the group and their community. The house is one of those masterpieces of creaking, curving spaciousness the Haight is filled with. Partially because of limited funds, but mostly because of the common consciousness that almost every group here adapts as its ethos, the Grateful Dead live and work together. They are the quintessential Bay Area band. Leader Jerry Garcia is a patron saint of the scene. Ken Kesey calls him "Captain Trips." There are no recordings of their music, which is probably just as well because no album could produce the feeling they generate in a dance hall. I have never seen them live, but I spent an evening at the Fillmore listening to tapes. The music hits hard and stays hard, like early Rolling Stones, but raw and open—more American. Theirs is the San Francisco sound. Nothing convoluted in the lyrics, just rock 'n' roll lingua franca. Not a trace of preciousness in the music, just funky chords. The big surprise about this music has nothing to do with electronics or some zany new camp. Performers in this city have knocked all that civility away. They are down in the dark, grainy roots.

Ask an aspiring musician from New York who his idols are and he'll begin a long list with the Beatles or Bob Dylan, then branch off into Paul Simon literacy or the Butterfield Blues bag or a dozen variations in harmonics and composition. Not so in San Francisco. Bob Dylan is like Christianity here; they worship but they don't touch. The sound of the Grateful Dead, or Moby Grape, or Country Joe and the Fish, is jug band music scraping against jazz. This evolution excludes most of the names in rock. A good band is a "heavy" band, a "hard" band.

Marty Balin, who writes for the Jefferson Airplane, declares: "The Beatles are too complex to influence anyone around here. They're a studio sound." Which is as close as a San Francisco musician comes to contempt. Their music, they insist, is a virgin forest, uncharted and filled with wildlife. This unwillingness to add technological effect is close to the spirit of folk music before Dylan electrified it. "A rock song still has to have drive and soul," Balin maintains. "Jazz started out as dance music, and ended up dead as something to listen to. If you can't get your effects live, the music's not alive."

Gary Duncan, lead guitarist for the Quicksilver Messenger Service, adds: "Playing something in a studio means playing for two months. Playing live, a song changes in performance. In a studio, you attack things intellectually; onstage it's all emotion."

San Francisco musicians associate Los Angeles with the evils of studio music. This is probably because almost every group has made the trek south to record. And the music available on record is anything but hard rock. A local band called Sopwith Camel earned everyone's disfavor with a lilting good-timey rendition of "Hello, Hello." "They give us a bad name," says one musician. "They're a diversion," says another. "They smile nice."

The rivalry between Northern and Southern California makes a cold war in pop inevitable. While musicians in Los Angeles deride the sound from up north as "pretentious and self-conscious" and shudder at the way "people live like animals up there," the Northern attitude is best summed up by a member of the Quicksilver Messenger Service who quipped: "L.A. hurts our eyes."

Part of the Holding Company puts down the Byrds because "they had to learn to perform after they recorded. Here, the aim is to get the crowd moving." A Jefferson Airplane says of the Beach Boys: "What Brian Wilson is doing is fine but in person there's no balls. Everything is prefabricated like the rest of that town. Bring them into the Fillmore, and it just wouldn't work."

The technology involved in putting on a light show doesn't seem to bother San Franciscans, however, because what they're really uptight about is not artificiality but Southern California. Even Ralph Gleason has little sympathy for the L.A. scene. "The freaks are fostered and nurtured by L.A. music hype," he says. "The hippies are different. What's going on here is natural and real."

The question of who is commercial and who is authentic is rhetorical. What really matters about San Francisco is what mattered about Liverpool three years ago. The underground occupies a pivotal place in the city's life. The Fillmore and the Avalon are jammed every weekend with beaded, painted faces and flowered shirts. The kids don't come from any mere bohemian quarter. Hip has passed the point where it signifies a commitment to rebellion. It has become the style of youth in the Bay Area, just as long hair and beat music were the Liverpool look.

San Francisco is a lot like that grimy English seaport these days. In 1964, Liverpool rang with a sound that was authentically expressive and the city never tried to bury it. This is what is happening in San Francisco today. The underground is open, unencumbered, and radiating. The rest of the country will get the vibrations soon.

Which everyone thinks is groovy. The Grateful Dead are willing to sing their 30-minute extravaganza, "Midnight Hour," for anyone who will listen, and if people pay, so much the better. But Bob Weir insists: "If the industry is gonna want us, they're gonna take us the way we are. If the money comes in, it'll be a stone gas."

It will be interesting to see what happens to San Francisco when the money men move in. It will be fascinating to watch the Fillmore become the Radio City Music Hall of rock. It will be a stone gas to take a Greyhound tour of the Haight. But that's another story about another time. Right now, give or take a little self-righteousness, this city is full of new ideas, new faces, and new music. The Liverpool of the West.

—1967

CHAPTER 9

Bell-Bottom Blue Jeans

I

EAST BERLIN—Everyone walks here. Because the shops close early, the cafes are expensive, and the cinemas few and far between, a popular pastime for young and old's the after-dinner stroll. The Unter Den Linden is a particularly suitable boulevard for this activity because it affords a commanding view of the Brandenburg Gate, now plugged up by the wire and concrete *anti-fascist shutwall*. Also, since the Unter Den Linden is only a few blocks away from Checkpoint Charlie, it is an excellent place to pick up radio from West Berlin.

Which brings us to Manfred. At 17, he is an accomplished cultural saboteur. Each night at 7:30 he stands in the Unter Den Linden, camouflaged by the crowds and the trees, and tunes in Armed Forces Radio. At 7:45 he is joined by a friend, Rolf. Both boys are dressed in *Mitteleuropa* mod. Rolf wears a loudly patterned shirt with a hand-sewn button-down collar. Manfred sports high shoes, longish hair, and bell-bottom blue jeans. The flared-leg effect is home-made, like almost everything he owns. Manfred's outfit is a pastiche of what is fashionable and what is available. Often this means shopping the back streets as well as the state-run stores.

At 7:55 Manfred adjusts his radio while Rolf looks up and down the street uneasily. But the cover is excellent. Besides, Rolf insists, at this time in East Berlin it is not difficult to hear American radio on the streets. That is because at 8:00 p.m. Armed Forces Radio begins to broadcast rock 'n' roll. It is not "the truth from the free world" that Manfred and Rolf are after. They want big-beat music. Pop music is much

more than a pastime here. Rock 'n' roll means The West.
And in East Berlin, teenagers don't have to burn draft cards
or smoke marijuana to rebel against the system. All they
have to do is tune in the radio.

Tonight's first song is "Hanky Panky." It seems ludicrous
against a background of posters the government has erected to
commemorate the fifth anniversary of the Wall. But Manfred
knows the words by heart. He sings along, in a strong southern
accent tempered by Germanic vowels.

Both boys are loyal followers of a group they call "Rollinkstone." Rolf is himself the drummer for an East German
combo called Die Kandles. The Anglicism is not surprising,
since it is fashionable for German groups to adapt English
names. Rolf and Manfred call themselves anti-Communists,
but ask Manfred why he hates the government and he points
to his scuffed shoes and the impossibly high price of his
jeans. And for Rolf, anti-Communism stems from the day
the police closed down the club in which Die Kandles were
playing.

For Rolf and Manfred, the culture we call adolescence exists
in miniature. A radio makes a handy status symbol, and
Manfred's is further enhanced by a small stuffed bear that
hangs from the antenna. There are portions of the Unter Den
Linden and surrounding avenues where unattached young
ladies make it a point to stroll. And there are still a few
clubs in East Germany where a teenager can feel like a
teenager.

The ABC, or Arthur Becker Clubhouse for *Jugen Talente* is
the spot where Rolf and Manfred make the scene. The bureau
in charge of Youth Kultur has located this cavern in a faraway
suburb, 30 minutes from the Unter Den Linden by S-Bahn. But
the ABC is one of the few places in East Berlin where pop
music as interpreted by amateur groups like Die Kandles can
be heard live. So each weekend Manfred and Rolf make the
trek. And tonight they offer to act as guides—in exchange for
a few West German marks.

We board the S-Bahn for Hirschgarten. From the station, we
walk down a long, unlit dirt road, skirting mud puddles and
wet grass, detouring through a field at one point to avoid an im-
patient dog. Two girls pass us in the opposite direction. They

warn of bees up ahead. Anyway, they say, ABC is closed tonight. Rolf begins to blame the government and Manfred insists that we proceed anyway. We lift camera and radio above the high grass and march through mud and shrubbery. Half expecting a force of security police to be awaiting us, we round a final bend, only to see lights and hear laughter.

Suddenly the doors burst open and shouting men and women spill into the dirt road. Led by a fully costumed bride and groom, they weave down the street in a wobbling bunny-line. Men toast each other, spilling Schnapps over their clothing. The women form a circle around the couple and clap, as the bride and groom dance, oblivious to the festivities. One particularly rosy-cheeked man walks toward us with an enormous mug of liquor, but we retreat into the woods to lick our wounds in private.

Manfred grumbles and Rolf translates: "He says they arranged the wedding now because they knew it was our time."

Within the hour we are back on the Unter Den Linden. There are the usual apologies, even a rhetorical offer to return the marks. But—okay, it's a story anyway. We say good night, but not before Manfred shakes his radio with enthusiasm. "Rollinkstone!" he screams. They disappear into the trees. But from their radio, Mick Jagger wails in Cockney fury:
I can't get no satisfaction
And I try . . . and I try . . .
I can't get no . . . No no no.

II

PRAGUE—In the late afternoon, they gather above the din of trams and pushcarts, at the top of Prague's main drag, Wenceslas Square. They sit where it is most conspicuous, like ashes on a carpet, along the steps leading to the National Museum.

They are beats. Some are students, some give change on street cars, and still others defy the law that requires universal labor or study. They comb their long hair, brush their jeans and cowboy jackets, and chant the pop liturgy as it was constructed in America 10 years ago.

61

Old people call them *manishkas*, an idiom formerly reserved for ugly girls. When they pass the museum, workers in knit overcoats or billowing overalls stop to stare and giggle. The Prague Spring has meant a melting of ice, making it that much easier to fall through. On the one hand, they can hear music on Radio Luxembourg or Radio Free Europe jam-free. But they cannot buy Western records in the shops. Authorities declare their willingness to sponsor American pop groups, but find the price for most acts prohibitive. And the biggest paradox for the beats is the government's attitude toward their existence. A visitor is informed that Prague is "modni" enough to sport stylish clothing, that it is "switched on" enough to sport a long-haired youth. But the kids themselves hear little of this bureaucratic praise. They are too busy running away from the cops, because in Prague, the elders sneer as they do anywhere, but the cops are part-time barbers.

So, when four plainclothesmen close in from either end of the museum, while a police van pulls up in the driveway, the kids scatter their playing cards and extinguish their cigarettes. Identity cards are surrendered and inspected. There are the usual questions about hair and idleness. The unofficial rule required beats to show their ears, so the more courageous began to wear their hair in pigtails or ponytails. Unsatisfied, the police seize three *manishkas*. The next day, they return sheepishly to the steps, their hair clipped to bristling crewcuts.

Petr Janda is long-haired and blue-jeaned, but he is in no danger of having his bangs clipped because they are a national asset. At 24, he is the lead guitarist and vocalist of Czechoslovakia's top pop group, the Olympiks. Though his face is craggy and his frame stooped, Janda is the one man in the C.S.R.—and one of the few in the Socialist world—who qualifies as an authentic pop star. He is the Local Product.

The son of a former judge who doubles on the violin in his spare time, Petr studied mechanics, and, after his secondary education, found himself working in Telephone Central, as a repairman. After three years, Janda quit to pursue full-time what he had been dabbling in since his school days: beat music. He added the magic of electricity to his old guitar by utilizing spare parts. And like countless teens (there are four professional beat groups in Czechoslovakia, but officials estimate that the amateur combos number between 300 and 500), he began to play with friends in small, peripatetic basement clubs. He signed with the Sputniks, who, in 1959, became the first pop group to be licensed by the Cultural Bureau. When the Sputniks split three years ago, Janda joined the newly forming Olympiks. The group has since recorded more than 30 songs. Their biggest hit, "Give Me More of Your Love," sold 40,000 discs—a smash by Czech standards.

Today, the Olympiks play nightly in their own club. Their fans sit politely at long formica tables, trying to ignore the chintzy wood paneling and the dour art that adorns the walls. There is smoking and clapping but no screaming in the audience. Because Petr Janda is a Czech, he can walk down the street with his clothing intact and his features unscarred. His fans are loyal, but unecstatic.

"All young people in Czechoslovakia are for American culture," he says. The Olympiks try to fill that need, vicariously. They wear a blue jean/black turtleneck uniform. Their repertory includes some original songs and some made famous by groups like the Stones, the Kinks, and the Animals. But they always sing in English. When Petr speaks English, his voice shakes as he grasps for equivalents, but he sings in a strong baritone:

I sleep through the day
I wake around four
But I always feel down
Never get off the floor
Till night comes around . . .
I'm feeling fine,
Midnight to six,
Well that's my time.

Hardly the image of smiling workers in a field of waving corn, their feet and hands dancing the dance of progress, hardly the Czechoslovakia you see on the back of coins. But Petr Janda says: "The Olympiks do not like the worker mentality." The four musicians who play with him snicker at his reference. "The workers are stupid," says Ladislav Klien, the rhythm guitarist. "They accept without questioning. They see you walk down the street, and they come up to touch your hair. They are laughing at your clothing or your girlfriend. Young people are very little fans for the Communists."

In Czechoslovakia, as in much of Eastern Europe, the government has undergone a discernible change in its attitude toward pop. Articles written during the late fifties decried this revisionism from the West, but that did little to loosen its hold, and in the early sixties, an official policy of peaceful coexistence was introduced. Twist lessons were given in Czech schools, and Elvis Presley—never enthusiastically greeted by the government—was at least acknowledged in print. Today, the government, through local culture centers, youth magazines, and the record company, Supraphon, has stepped into the pop business with a vengeance. Its aim seems to be the production of groups to rival those in the West. Radio Prague plays pop—East and West—every afternoon. Concerts to determine which groups can receive professional status are held annually here, as in Poland and Hungary.

The Olympiks happen to be the foremost expression of the Czech pop style. "We are not popular in the high office," Jan Anthpacak, the drummer, notes. But though all beat groups must play before a culture commission twice a year to renew their licenses, the Olympiks have never encountered any trouble. They are the only group in Czechoslovakia to travel abroad. Karel Svoboda, who writes and sings for Mefisto, another leading group, says he receives 60 crowns (16 to the dollar) for a disc, and 125 for a performance. Only 1 percent of the profits on a record go to the artists and writers: 99 percent go to the state. The Olympiks are better paid, but even they are aware that their equivalents in other countries are worshiped not only by the fans, but by the banks.

Now the group swings seriously into rehearsal, while from the balcony, a cleaning woman and repairman watch in stunned disbelief. Once onstage, the Olympiks undergo an electronic transformation. Their accents and mannerisms fade into the music. When they sing "Help," they are the Beatles. When they jump into "Sunny Afternoon," they become the Kinks. It is only during the breaks, when Ladislav screams about the quality of percussion or vocal, that the musicians become, again, kids from Prague. Ladislav is the fanatic. "When I was a student," he says, "my father didn't let me hear music. So naturally, I learned to play it. Now, the money is good."

Petr Janda agrees. The money is good. He dresses himself and his 21-year-old fiance, Jana, in the latest Czech mod gear. When she comes to the club, she wears a peacoat, jersey pullover, and tweed skirt. She usually brings—along with her broad grin—a few bottles of Czech beer (very good) or Czech cola (very bad) for the boys. Jana has a few questions for any American she meets: What is a Lovin' Spoonful? When will we end the war in Vietnam? What does Coca Cola taste like? Petr asks after the health of Allen Ginsberg, whom he met when the poet stopped in Prague last year. And do they wear miniskirts in New York? And why do they say the new Beatles album is different?

Behind the questions is the question: What is America like? There are still cities in the world where words like "New York" open eyes wide, and Prague is one of those places. The image on both sides is distorted; the Olympiks see and sing America through a glass, very darkly.

—1967

CHAPTER 10

Je Fais Comme Je Veux

NEW YORK—In Holland and Denmark, where English is widely spoken, songs in the mother tongue rarely make the charts these days. Throughout most of Europe, Anglo-American hits are reworked by local stars. Germany became one of the few nations (along with South Africa) to dig "The Ballad of the Green Berets" when the song was released in English by Barry Sadler and in German under the title "One Hundred Men and One Command," by a local artist. Both discs were hits.

But in France, few American songs reach the charts. There are exceptions: recent smashes include "These Boots Were Made for Walking" and a song little known in its native America, called "Juanita Banana." As recorded by the Peels, this novelty item about a Mexican peasant whose daughter becomes an off-key opera star was taken to heart by the French. All over the Riviera this summer, bikinied boppers sang the refrain of "Juanita Banana," which is a deliberately distorted aria. The song was released in four separate versions, each a smash.

Basically, *la gloire française* manifests itself in the business of francifying Americana. The French don't idolize Elvis Presley; they invent one of their own—a chap named Johnny Halliday. And now, with the influx of beatniks into Paris, the men in the echo chambers have come up with a *clochard* saint for the yeh-yehs to adore. His hair is long, his shirt flowered, his jeans and army fatigues dusty, his boots scuffed, and his guitar—in the best folksinger tradition—is spanking new and expensive.

His name is Antoine and his biggest hit, "Les Elucubrations d'Antoine" has sold over a million discs, making the 22-year-old engineering student the hottest pop commodity this side of the Maginot line. Antoine sings what his promo-men call *"le protest."* He orders the president to stock birth control pills in all pharmacies. He crows: "Je fais comme je veux." He cuts on war, violence, and adulthood. His heart is with the Beats on the Ile de la Cité, and his material is aimed at those who cannot understand the words Bob Dylan is singing. Anyone who can imagine "The Times They Are a-Changin' " and "Hard Rain's Gonna Fall" in simplified French has heard Antoine sing.

The most interesting thing about the myth of Antoine is not the voice or face behind it, but the imitators trying to Xerox the carbon copy. In "Elucubrations" (nonsense talk) Antoine blithely suggested that Johnny Halliday was old-fashioned and should be put on display. Halliday responded with a stinging put-down, "Cheveux longs et idées courtes." Stepping cautiously into the fray, to avoid stumbling over his hair, which hangs down to his knees, a newcomer named Edouard took still another swipe, in a hit song called "Hallucination." Antoine sued, but the French CBS record complex kept the publicity coming by carefully masking the identity of Edouard (virtually hidden under all that hair). Rumors flew—was it Johnny Halliday in drag? While Antoine fumed, the mysterious Edouard let loose another blast: "N'ai pas peur, Antoinette."

• • •

Style met style recently when New York City played host to none other than Antoine himself. To celebrate the signing of an American contract, Warner Brothers flew their ersatz Bob Dylan across the ocean to participate in a "10-hour New York protest." The host for the nonstop happening was Andy Warhol, silver haired, dark shaded, leather jacketed. Antoine's escort for the day, Nico, met the superstar at the airport with a bouquet of bananas.

Assembling a following of press and groupies was not difficult. Editors of fan magazines brought their cameras; fashion reporters tagged along with open sketch pads; *Paris Match* and *France Soir* came along for the ride. The public relations gestalt assembled at command in the lobby of the Warwick Hotel. Cameras popped and pencils scribbled as Antoine boarded an "authentic" autobus rented from a real French restaurant for the occasion. The doorway was festooned with balloons; posters along the side announced: "Antoine is here."

"Who the hell is he?" a Con Ed worker mumbled, but his observation was lost. There are two ways to create a happening. One is to let it happen. The other is to invite the press and hope for the best fabrications in print. Warhol, master of the first, stood poised behind the dark glasses, and turned the dials on the second.

First stop: Paraphernalia. Betsy Johnson is all smiles. Come try on my buckles and chrome. Antoine changes into blue velvet, Nico into a lavender jumpsuit. Snap. Crackle. Pop. Antoine in his mod gear does not look anything like a 22-year-old student with a Ph.D. in engineering. But the merchants of novelty search in weird corners for that certain something NEW. Antoine comes on as too nice a guy to put down. The one aspect of the Dylanesque personality that he hasn't learned to imitate is a cagey evasive quality where the press is concerned. As for the Dylanesque quality of the lyrics, they speak for themselves:

My best friend, if you knew him
You wouldn't be able to stay away
The other day he wasn't very bright
He took a laxative instead of taking the train.

Antoine's hair curls mercilessly around his ears. His nose is long and pudgy. His lanky frame fits easily into the new Betsy Johnson male look. Two young girls, attracted by the crowds, stop to see what the commotion is about. They are French—touring with their parents, out shopping on the chic East Side. They see HIM surrounded by tinfoil models. "Antoine! Antoine!" they scream. Real tears make riverbeds in their makeup. "Le foto, le foto," they shout. In dinner-table English, they explains his fascination to a fawning press: "If he wasn't Antoine, he'd be so ugly."

The day passes with a series of such occurrences. At the Janis Gallery a happening is canceled when the police decide that the showroom is too crowded with erotic-art groupies for Antoine's party to enter. At the Factory, which is embellished with bananas for the occasion, Andy presents Antoine with a huge stick-on banana. Antoine smiles a crooked, puzzled grin. Cameras click. Time for his screen test. They sit Antoine before a dark scrim and tell him to hold as still as possible. Andy starts his camera, focuses, and lets the machine run itself. Antoine is puzzled again. Fifteen minutes go by. No one is paying attention. Antoine's smile wanes. The man from UPI says: "Mr. Warhol, would you hold up that banana. Mr. Warhol, will you show us how it works. How does the banana work, Mr. Warhol?"

Antoine is yawning, but the day is nowhere near over. Antoine would like some pommes frites and vin ordinaire, but there is a Zen Buddhist dinner at the Paradox. Antoine would like to go shopping for rhythm and blues records but there is a "protest" meeting with the Fugs and a jam session with the Byrds.

Like the song says: *je fais comme je veux.*

God help us when French psychedelic music is born.

—1966

CHAPTER 11

Ravi and the Teenie Satori

NEW YORK—They are waiting for him in the glass-enclosed library of Asia House, over coffee, cream, and croissants. All the regulars are there: the reporter in her tweedsuit uniform nibbles gingerly on a breakfast bun. A tall angular gentleman is delivering his prerecorded monologue about last summer's visit to Madras. Two Indians in mercantile mufti are warbling metaphysics: "One must live alone to survive in the modern world." And a Day-Glo journalist, lean and oozing television, stops a hostess in swirling sari and demands: "Spell that—will ya?" She answers with a caress in her voice: "S-i-t-a-r."

He walks in, hands neatly folded like two starched handkerchiefs under his chin, beige muslin tunic over creased black pants, hair in neat curls over his collar. In the corner of the room, two reporters from *Datebook* magazine are fiddling with a Brownie camera and a tape recorder. With glitter in their eyes, and clucking fan noises on their lips, they approach the master to ask their timid question.

"Whatdya think of George?"

TV-face butts in with a 21-inch grin. "Mr. Shanker, I'm pleased t'meet ya." The sweet face smiles back in non-recognition. To his right, the angular gentleman is recounting autumn in Darjeeling; to his left the tweed lady is discussing the feasibility of a mini-sari. But *Datebook's* microphone is hovering above his teacup, so he answers into it: "I have accepted George as my disciple. He is not at all like other pop musicians. But I have nothing to do with him as a Beatle."

The girls from *Datebook* smile thank you before they are pushed away by an Asia House question about the evolution

of the tabla in the "raga sound." Back in their corner, one
of them observes: "He's got such soft hands to shake." And
a high school girl, doing a term paper on the star, answers:
"He's a lot cuter than Ali [Akbar Khan]."

He is Ravi Shankar, India's crown jewel in the coffers of
world music. He is in New York to give three concerts at
Philharmonic Hall, and to accept a citation from the India
Council and a long list of related organizations for "dis-
tinguished achievement in creating and advancing American
interest in Indian music and culture."

At 46, he has watched and heard and touched the Western
world as no Eastern musician before him. He wrote those
piercing death screams into Satyajit Ray's Apu trilogy, as
well as the music for a British TV production of *Alice In
Wonderland*. He can hold his own with jazz or jam with
Yehudi Menuhin. His American audience is centered in
cities and college towns—wherever the culturati cavort.
Ravi Shankar has been Martian-in-residence for years. He
says: "It gives me great pleasure to see people without any
background in our music appreciating it." He does object
to ads like the one Columbia records placed in his concert
program, advising the curious to take a peek at the folk
sounds of India ("After all," soothes the copy, "a little
Eastern exposure never hurt anyone.") "I do not play folk
or primitive songs," he declares. "This is classical music."

Ravi Shankar stands untouched amid all that grasping splendor. He neither accepts nor rejects the adulation, but watches
it all with ice-and-fire eyes. He wears the expression of a
man who has been complimented many times for speaking
English well, even though it is his nation's official language.
He reaches out for a cookie, a handshake, or a question
with a subtle sobriety. His "new" audience responds with
all the garlands it usually throws its admirers, but without
the frenzy. After all, he doesn't even play rock 'n' roll.
He merely influences, stealthily, cryptically. He encourages
by merely tolerating. Like a pop star, he gives off light
without warmth.

During his concerts, Philharmonic Hall brimmed with the
sought-after satori. Seated on an Indian carpet, and surrounded
with wafting incense, Ravi Shankar stroked and patted this

weird giraffe of an instrument they call a sitar. He tickled its belly and rubbed its back. His bare feet, knotted at rest, kept the rhythm. When the concert had ended, and the lobby overflowed with peacoats and passion, everyone seemed embarrassed at how truly nonexclusive the raga has become. Even a year ago, you could lose yourself amid all the cigarette-holder suave at one of these affairs. The very rebellion against slick that once drove hippies to purist folk sounds now puts them into raga. Hip has become masscult, and Ravi Shankar finds himself not the prophet of an elite, but the universal guru. His following wants Buddhahood on a long-play record. Tao on tap, a bath in the Ganges without getting wet. And they want Ravi Shankar to sock it to them.

But he is no saran-wrap swami. "I have nothing to do with raga-rock," he declares. But he does not reject the form. "I do not think this music is ruining the sitar. It is like the guitar which is used by classical musicians and also for folk and now popular music."

On the tenuous connection between acid rock and raga, he says: "I have met a number of people who have been studying or indulging in that field. They are absolutely sure I am high whenever I play. I have never had any drug experience. I can only say, through use of discipline and yoga, drugs are not needed."

Ravi Shankar's pivotal place in the teenie underground became assured last year when George Harrison named him personal mentor. The master was not so sure at first that he wanted the honor. He met George at a dinner party last June. Though he had heard for some time that the Beatles were among his most ardent English admirers, he refused to consider their patronage anything more than a "gimmick." But he found Harrison "humble and sincere; he said he wanted to learn properly and I told him he must give up everything and start again from basics." George surprised everyone by following through on the suggestion, and he arrived in India complete with a bushy moustache. But the disguise proved inadequate. Every day, his bemused teacher noted 2,000 to 5,000 teenagers screaming for their idol outside the hotel. Enraged, Harrison held a press conference to berate Indian youth for turning their backs on native music. Delighted elders had the text reprinted in all the papers; and suddenly the Beatles became tradition-alists.

Harrison's conversion has given Ravi Shankar access to the elite in American pop music. He seems delighted at the reception but unwilling to reciprocate. Western musicians have not taught him anything, he insists. "The worlds of jazz, folk, and electronic music have all been influenced by our music because they found something they didn't already have. But Western music hasn't influenced me at all. We are so very much richer."

Ravi Shankar greets the great glance Eastward by glancing back. He is willing to play for deaf audiences who cry "bravo" anyway. He is willing to sip coffee with tweedy creatures from the press. He is willing to teach musicians what raga is all about. And he is willing to confront this latest frenzy, which calls itself a teenager, with the ease of somebody who has been where everything is going all along.

The teenie satori makes him smile. Five years ago, a lot of people thought his music sounded like a sick cat; now he packs 'em in in London and New York. Five years ago, they wondered why he didn't wear a turban; now they ask for his autograph. Five years ago, they called it an "ethnic" sound; now they write term papers about him and talk in hushed whispers about his vital infusion of rock 'n' roll.

Ravi Shankar smiles from the corners of his mouth, and tells those reporters gathered to hear his pronouncements about their youth: "Touch wood, we haven't had to borrow from other cultures. Our music grows within itself."

—1967

CHAPTER 12

Giraffe Hunters

NEW YORK—Shapes of things:
Connie De Nave holds a press conference for the Yardbirds (fresh from England) in the Americana Hotel's Provence Room. See—gold provincial wallpaper—that's how it got its name.

Amid the noncrystal chandeliers, the Miami Beach miasma, reporters fire sugary questions at the boys in the Chelsea Antiques Market gear.

Jeff Beck tells us how: "Each of us has his own scene inside his head when we play."

Chris Dreja reveals: "The Carnaby scene is a drag. People realize that whatever they buy—even if it's fresh from the shop—they'll walk down the street and see everyone wearing it."

Reporters cluster around the customary liquor cart in back of the room. Connie De Nave herself puts down the immigration authorities for refusing to consider the Yardbirds unique. The lady reporters size the boys up, and the boys respond with winks and Buster Brown grins.

Keith Relf wins most of the votes for his groupie story: "I had 15 letters from a girl after I told some reporters I liked rhubarb crumble, which is a kind of fruitish pudding. She said she was the best rhubarb crumble maker going. I had people write her and say I was married; I tried everything but she kept writing, saying I had to eat her rhubarb crumble."

The methodic sound of scribbling. "What finally happened?" The answer is lost in another question. The press conference ends that way—as uneventful, as precooked, as soppy as a "fruitish pudding".

This week's reality is a lot like that dismal affair. It stares brazenly at you over coffee and danish when the conversation turns to squinting whispers over an up 'n' coming guitarist slated for a major piece that month. Your informer's eyes narrow, she sips her tea between syllables, and explains in perfect journalese: "That, my dear, is a hard cock to follow."

Reality rings every weekday morning at 10:00 a.m., in a parade of coiffed agents and spangled promo-men who sing the praises of clients on one hand, and offer gifties—FREE FREE FREE—on seven others. The Swarthmore voice confides: "I just had to tell you we're holding a private luncheon, dear, for Peter Noone, and I know you'd . . ."

The real interview: his press agent sits alongside a pile of printed bios—the letterhead bears the greeting: GNUS FOR YOUSE. He grooms and coaxes a budding superstar with combing strokes in his voice. "Tell Dick about the time you slipped Bobby Dylan an exploding cigar . . . you'll really find this story groovy, Dick, I know you will."

In the real world, little red dots tell you which records to watch. In the real world, the crooner of candy-cane ballads is sleeping with his son. In the real world, Dick Clark smiles a sour-cream grin over a pack of bad-breath mints while the Action Kids turn cartwheels over a song about racial discontent masquerading as a cha-cha. The radio station that won't play music that advocates taking "toxins" distributes a record magazine with a "psychedelic special." Very real.

God may be dead. Reagan may win in California. It may finally be proven that a steady exposure to flashing lights and deafening music causes cancer of the coccyx. No matter—they will keep churning out The Sound. Like the old man says: between the idea and the reality, between the motion and the act, falls the shadow.

This week's reality is all in the shade.

Who makes a superstar? Who makes a trend? Which makes an art form? Who connects desire with spasm, and meshes need with product? Who tells the kids under the el in Astoria what to sing? Who fills Plato's cave with Martha and the Vandellas? Why are the same kids who ring the registers over acid rock sound lapping up Paul Revere and the Raiders? It's like eating beef Stroganoff with frozen wonton soup, but the kids don't seem to be getting indigestion. The question is—who taught them to eat like that in the first place?

What's next? Barrio-rock, blue-blood bluegrass, a chamber orchestra playing Chuck Berry, Kate Smith eating avocados? When I find out, I'll tell. If I don't, I'll guess anyway.

In college, they showed us an anthropology film about a tribe in Africa somewhere. In the middle of a ferocious famine, the men had to go out hunting giraffes, with water slung over their shoulders, and singing, walking for arid days, trying to smell giraffe dung in the clouds, until finally, over a distant ridge, they saw just the neck of an enormous giraffe with spots like brown eyes. As it smelled them its feet churned and its neck waved panicky in the wind—glorious in color—but the men whooped, shook their singing bolos overhead, and ran after the animal; it leaping, careening, and the men tossing their weapons at the animal's legs—legs spread apart for distance—until, hit once, again, it fell straight on its head like the log of the century, fell on its face, waiting, and as the men slashed with their knives, the animal's eyes closed slowly, heavily, lids quivering. When they had sliced it up—they show you this in the film—they ate the testicles for power and then they filled their gourds with blood and slung the hollow animal on poles over their shoulders, and when they marched back to the village there was a feast for days and the giraffe's head, still proud and sleek, adorned the chief's hut as a trophy.

Rock 'n' roll is the giraffe. Public relations men, disc jockeys, emcees, executives, socko boffo copy boys, fabulous blondes, prophets, frauds, fakes, connect-the-dots copies, and under-assistant West Coast promo-men hunt with their snares and bolos, cut, castrate, slice up the meat, and hang shaggy heads in trophy.

I love the giraffe for its color, its coat, and its bobbing neck. I love to watch it run. So I never watch when it falls, and it falls all the time. People like me are good at loving giraffes, but can't save them. That's up to you.

And that's this week's reality.

—1966

77

PART II

The Mystique

CHAPTER 13

The Psychedelic Psell

NEW YORK—Okay.

You've swallowed the magic cube, downed a cup of "organic" tea with filigree leaves, and placed the diamond stereo needle on the appropriate acid sounds.

Now sit back and wait 20 minutes, until twinges of nausea herald the coming of the hereafter.

Meanwhile, ponder this:

A discotheque advertises: "psychedelic beauty contests" on WMCA. Admen chortle: "Don't blow your cool—blow your mind." Bosley Crowther calls *The Fantastic Voyage* "quite a trip." Albert Zugsmith's successor to *Fanny Hill* is a movie called *LSD—I Hate You*. They photographed *Kaleidoscope* in "psychedelic color." *The Cabinet of Dr Caligari* is advertised by the McBurney Y in last week's *Voice* as: "The original psychedelic filmic trip."

Psychedelic shoes. Acid ads. LSD greeting cards. Mandala shopping bags. As the music sharpens into neon and the room thickens into tapioca, ask yourself this: What about the prophet's profits?

Timothy Leary's name appears in a mass-circulation magazine or two every week. His records are being rushed to outlets all over the country. He turns out introductions to other people's books the way the Japanese produce tin Statues of Liberty. Currently, he's writing his memoirs. In a white shirt, white jeans, and white sneakers, he brings his calm charisma to *The Merv Griffin Show*. He holds press conferences at the Advertising Club on Park Avenue. And, if half the rumors are true, he turns on doctors, lawyers, publishers, and—by his own implication—Presidents-to-be.

When the feds chose to arrest Leary for leaving the country while under indictment as a "narcotics offender," they
merely convinced thousands of people that the place to be
on Tuesday nights is the Village Theatre, where he hosts his
Psychedelic Celebrations. The government is Leary's most
generous patron; it showers him with publicity. Now that
he swings with the beautiful people, the feds are helping
Leary reach the folks who guzzle beer.

Along Second Avenue, Leary acknowledges the greetings of
admirers like a Zen Nelson Rockefeller. He folds his hands
together and bows his head in the direction of a compliment.
His eyes close slightly; his mouth spreads in a quiescent
comprehensive smile.

In the delicatessen on 7th Street, a middle-aged waitress
recognizes the Doctor and dries her hands on an apron to
serve him. "Have I got a pastrami sandwich for you," she
chortles. When it arrives, she thrusts it toward him with a
flourish, and, as Leary pours his beer, takes it back again.
"Who gave you that corned beef?" she scowls. "Pastrami is
juicier; you get pastrami."

Leary munches his sandwich and begins his spiel: "It's going
to take at least one generation to come to terms with LSD."

The waitress beams.

"This is a transition generation. When you think of the history
of new movements, no culture has been so tolerant of a force
that's going to wipe it out as America. In any other time or
place we'd be in danger of our lives."

The cook comes out of his kitchen for a peek.

"Imagine an LSD revolution in China."

Any journalist who listens to Leary's quiet assurances of
triumph ("The police state mentality always attempts to repress
sensory experience; it never works"), his plans ("Our design is
to educate as well as turn on . . . we open in California this
January"), and his awareness ("Any form of energy can be
misused by fools and villains. We're trying to teach people
to take it seriously; the average man has got to come to
his senses") faces a formidable problem. In a city of gilded
hoaxes, are the hair that falls graying over Timothy Leary's
eyes, the round green marble eyes, the encrusted bird dung on
his sweater—all part of the hype?

Reaching Dr. Leary for an interview is no longer as easy as dialing 914 and asking Information for the League for Spiritual Discovery. But it's easy enough to pop into the theater on Tuesday afternoon, when the League holds dress rehearsals. Workmen sweep in the aisles, oblivious to the Revolution. The theater's baroque cherubs and flourishes frame the visual fireworks onstage. It's like looking at an orange in a hand-carved mahogany crate.

"The theater has been taken over by careerist intellectuals," Leary says. "It has to be returned to its original motive. Plays by Tennessee Williams, for instance, are the memoirs of a neurotic, not art. Art must involve the senses. All original drama is psychedelic. The theater, remember, was originally a religious experience. It all stems back to religious motives—someone with a vision turns other people on. That's why we're proud to be packing 'em in down here."

What's packing them in is *The Death of the Mind*, a mixed-media meditation on that psychedelic icon, the Steppenwolf. Leary's associates, Jackie Cassen and Rudi Stern, took five months to create the visuals. They worked with a miniature theater at Millbrook, using fifteen machines and a series of complexly painted slides and mandalas. Rudi Stern says of his work in intermedia: "What we're doing is a return to basic forms in theater, to shadow play. Artaud first envisioned a theatre taking the form of mythic structure—light, sound, and shadow replacing narrative, pantomime replacing acting. It's all a very pure thing."

Getting the point of a Cassen-Stern light show is entirely a matter of association. Bring along that old linear thinking, and you'll be baffled, if not bored. If that sounds like Marshall McLuhan, it's no accident. "McLuhan knows about psychedelic art," Leary says, "but he's all external; he hasn't seen the inside yet. It'll be fascinating to see what happens when he finally takes LSD."

This may be just a case of academic envy, but perhaps the day will come when taking acid is essential to understanding media, not to mention music, slang, and interior decoration. What with acid art in the museums, acid rock on the radio, and acid chatchkas in the boutiques, Leary could become instant Americana. It's probably not his fault that enlightenment will come for most of us in the form of a lava-light. But what kind of spiritual revolution hinges on the material, and why does it have to be commerce that converts?

Jackie Cassen protests: "We don't consider this commercialized. This has nothing to do with distribution. We're involved in a religious celebration here." But Cassen and Stern reproduce the psychedelic experience in some very secular churches. They did the lighting for the Byrds' latest gig at the Gate. *Time* magazine calls their work "boffo." And a large ad in *Variety* boasts: "They can convert any room into a kaleidoscopic world of movement, light, and color (and they'll do it so you've got enough left over in your budget for a new set of China). They can turn a sagging club into the hottest spot in town . . . Jackie Cassen and Rudi Stern [available] for discotheques, fashion shows, ballet, industrial shows, commercials, bar mitzvahs."

Kinetic kreplach? Mind-manifesting matzoh? The Doctor has until the first psychedelic Ban Roll On commercial to do something about all this.

—1967

CHAPTER 14

Maharishi Meets the Press

NEW YORK—The Maharishi Mahesh Yogi arrived in New York last Thursday, fresh from triumphs in all the pop capitals of the West. The Beatles sent pink tulips and carnations to his suite at the Plaza. The Beach Boys, long fascinated by mystic meditation, accompanied him from Los Angeles. And the New York press establishment greeted him with equal measures of suspicion and relief. They were, after all, tired of the hippies.

On Friday morning, he received reporters in the Plaza's State Suite, a generous room decorated in Versailles nouveau. Chic ladies and gentlemen from the fashion slicks scurried around television cables for a glimpse of the guru's smile. The ballsier reporters squatted around a white satin couch on which the Maharishi reclined.

He is a practical man. That is the only defense he offers for his meditative technique. "Maybe, it works," the Maharishi shrugs at the end of a lecture, leaving his audience to ponder their needs and alternatives. In organizing his Spiritual Regeneration Movement, he has shown the same sense of transcendental pragmatism. While his eventual plans call for universal participation, he extends an immediate invitation to the "fortunate possessors of resources." He wants to train one teacher for every population of 100,000. This network of subgurus would be composed almost entirely of people who are powerful, important, or rich.

The Maharishi makes no attempt to disguise his elitism. He considers wealth and achievement important signs of spiritual advancement. Success, he reasons, is the logical result of inner peace, and failure cannot occur except through inner strife. Thus, he who is wealthy is usually healthy and potentially wise.

Wherever he has gone, the Maharishi has taken his movement to the tastemakers. In London, he found the Beatles; in San Francisco, the Grateful Dead. When he brought his technique to Germany, factory bosses embraced the movement after they discovered that transcendental meditation could increase production. In New York, the Maharishi wanted to meet the media. A large theatrical agency, which also handles public relations for the Ringling Brothers, Barnum & Bailey Circus, arranged his press conference, circulated in the audience with flowers in their stiff lapels, and surrounded their client like steel-gray columns.

"Jesus didn't have any public relations men around him," noted one reporter. "That is why he took so many hundreds of years to be known," the Maharishi replied in a small, tinkling voice. He cradled a hyacinth bud in one hand and gestured with the other. His eyes shone under the klieg lights.

"Your Holiness, do you ever suffer?"

"I don't remember the last time I was depressed."

"Your Holiness, nine years ago you left your hermit's cave in the Himalayas. Why did you leave?"

"To come out."

"Your Majesty, how old are you?"

"As you look at me."

"What do your beads symbolize? What did you do for the Beatles? Was your father a wise man?"

"He must have been."

"What did he do?"

"Work . . . as all men."

"Ahh, he's not gonna tell you."

The Maharishi does not enjoy talking about himself. When a personal question arises, his smile dims to a perplexed frown. He usually circumvents his own history, but he is reported to be about 56 years old, the son of a government revenue collector named Mahesh (Maharishi means great sage, and a yogi is a teacher). He is a university graduate who worked in a factory before he became a holy man.

In recent days, his cave has been replaced by a palatial ashram with soundproof walls and indirect lighting. Such luxuriance has caused widespread resentment against the Maharishi among India's holy men. As has his place under the pleasure dome. He does seem to approve of any action that brings fulfillment ("If we are given the ability to have desires," he says, "why should we not also have the right to realize them?"). He rebukes religious leaders for their attempts to dogmatize experience ("Control has been found damaging to life. It is opposed to evolution and change"). And a hefty chunk of his lecture is always devoted to reconciling spiritual with material gain ("How is it possible for a man not to be material; the whole body is material").

But this unstructured approach does not extend to the Maharishi's personal system of meditation, which is a ritualized, abstract procedure. His most publicized accomplishment has been the conversion of acidheads (something neither Billy Graham nor the narcs could achieve). Although he has never suggested that drugs are evil (only unnecessary), his followers seem to relish the "evolutionary" aspects of turning straight. Audiences at his talks are urged not to smoke. If that doesn't sound like the bidding of a closet hedonist, neither does vegetarianism, and yet the Maharishi eats no meat.

Though he ministers to the elect, he vehemently denies an interest in amassing personal wealth. Questions about money make him almost sad. After a few jibes from the press last Friday, he quipped: "I am a monk and a monk has no pockets." But the reporters chose to dwell on mercenary matters, and their concern was not entirely unprovoked. With a chuckle in his voice, the Maharishi answered a random question about poverty in India by explaining that the poor were lazy. A soft gasp—something like the deflation of a helium balloon—followed when he added: "The hungry of India, China, anywhere, are lazy because of their lack of self-knowledge. We will teach them to derive from within, and then they will find food."

In the back of the room, a reporter with a sleek razor cut and a yellow rose in his lapel pondered the dynamics of transcendental deprivation. "Do we have to ignore the poor to achieve inner peace?" he asked.

"Like a tree in the middle of a garden, should we be liberal and allow the water to flow to other trees, or should we drink ourselves and be green?"

"But isn't this selfish?"

"Be absolutely selfish. That is the only way to bring peace, to be selfish, and if one does not have peace, how is one to help others attain it?"

With a smile and a syllogism, he was kindling his own pyre. The cynic's mask reporters wear so well slipped easily over most of the faces in that room after the Maharishi revealed that he was "no more interested in Vietnam than anywhere else in the world." He called Lyndon Johnson a peacemaker, to the imperceptible slamming of inner doors. A public relations man hastily called an end to the questioning just as the Maharishi announced that the Beach Boys would accompany him on his next nationwide tour.

But the Maharishi's press reception says more about our own preconceptions of holy men from the East than it does about the value of transcendental meditation. Do we have the right to demand that our gurus be democrats as well? Are we so certain that Jesus was a socialist?

What is disturbing is not the Maharishi's Dale Carnegie approach to the politics of salvation. A teacher who has found the truth seldom worries about the context in which it is pronounced. But his followers—the rock stars, post-hippies, and ex-radicals—must take the blame for letting "truth" come before reality. They must know that this country is facing its most impolite summer in more than 100 years. Are we to teach the National Guard bliss-consciousness so they can perform their duties with inner peace? Are we to meditate between strafings? Can we ever transcend America?

That's the solution this year's guru offers. His message is one we are desperate to believe: that guilt is a futile emotion. "My heart is bouncing with bliss," he said last Sunday to a capacity crowd at the Felt Forum. "It is this afternoon that I am to announce that without a doubt, transcendental meditation, if carried throughout the world, will create peace for generations to come."

His audience of teenyboppers and matrons who had seen him on Johnny Carson sighed and smiled at the small man amid the chrysanthemums. A middle-aged lady in a see-through dress and white go-go boots folded her hands in gratitude.

—1967

CHAPTER 15

A Quiet Evening at the Balloon Farm

NEW YORK—Mixed media. Lots of light. Noise enough to make your ears sing back. Blows the mind.

Okay, a discotheque. But what's with this balloon farm thing?

Bob Dylan named it. You're supposed to figure out what it means to you.

Inside, there's this couple. Dancing. The girl, in a paisley shift and tree-bark stockings, seems to be moving to some internal rhythm. Her partner is bathed in light: electric blue. He swings low, encircling her waist without touching. His tongue darts snakelike toward her hips, retreating as she grinds forward. The girl takes off her glasses and hands them to her partner. She swoops as the walls play a strobe-lit threnody. Wow—you don't see that stuff on *Hullabaloo*.

The dance is called the Gobble. It started on the Lower East Side. Now they're grinding it out in Forest Hills. But the Gobble can be done anywhere. Which is fortunate, because the Balloon Farm is not your average rock 'n' ravage joint. The place has atmosphere. Originally called the Dom (which is Polish for "home"), it's a huge, mirrored ballroom where generations of immigrants came to dance, drink, and maybe find a little affection. The men's rooms still retain that compelling stench of beer and sausage. The dance floor is scuffed from the pounding of a million stomping polkas. Even though hippies have made St. Mark's Place their drag, the old gestalt lingers on, haunting the Balloon Farm with the irony of tradition.

Which brings us to Andy Warhol. This is Andy's club, so it shows his movies. On one screen, a lady who is possibly a man munches away on a ripe banana. On another screen, they have tied someone to a chair and are putting cigarettes out in his nose, winding belts around his neck, and fitting a tight leather mask over his face.

That's called *Vinyl*. Its creator is sitting quietly in the balcony. He is working the projector, pensive and subdued in his black chino/polo shirt/leather jacket uniform. Mirror sunglasses make his eyes totally inaccessible. His hair is straight, bright silver.

"Hi," he says.

"Who's the guy in the film?" you ask.

"Henry."

"Henry who?"

"Geldzahler."

"Beautiful."

He turns back to the projector, his fingers shuffling tins of film. Strobe lights crackle like horsewhips around him. ("When it looks like they're enjoying it, he makes it all go faster," someone near me offers.) Onstage, Gerard Malanga grabs a roll of phosphorescent tape and wraps it around his partner and himself. Handed a whip, he snaps it in time to the strobes. As a finale, he smothers his body in yellow paint and grabs a purple spotlight, which makes him glow and deepens the shadow around his eyes and teeth. Speed zone. He untangles two blinking strobe lights and swings them around his hips, sending violent, stabbing rays into the audience. ("At least he didn't piss on us," I heard a teenybopper whisper. Her friend grumbled, "They said he would, too.")

For the next ten minutes, electricity becomes a weapon of frontal assault. Bulbs blink patterns onto the ceiling and the mirrored walls. Those two portable strobes make your entire line of vision sway. It's all very much like sitting stoned in the middle of a Christmas tree on speed.

Which brings us to the Velvet Underground, Andy's rock group. Sometimes they sing, sometimes they just stroke their instruments. Their sound is a savage series of atonal thrusts and electronic feedback. Their lyrics combine sadomasochistic frenzy with free-association imagery. The whole thing seems to be the product of a secret marriage between Bob Dylan and the Marquis de Sade.

Andy says he is through with phosphorescent flowers and cryptic soup cans. Now it's rock. He may finally conquer the world through its soft, teenage underbelly.

"It's ugly," he admits. "It's a very ugly effect when you put it all together. But it's beautiful. You know, you just look at the whole thing—the Velvets playing and Gerard dancing and all the film and light, and it's a beautiful thing. Very Vinyl. Beautiful."

"Yeah, beautiful. There are beautiful sounds in rock. Very lazy, dreamlike noises. You can forget about the lyrics in most songs. Just dig the noise, and you've got our sound. We're putting everything together—lights and din and music—and we're reducing it to its lowest common denominator. We're musical primitives."

That's John Cale. He plays a mean, slashing viola. And piano, when he has to. He and Lou Reed once shared a three-room flat on Ludlow Street and a group called the Primitives. Bassman Sterling Morrison recalls: "Sometimes we'd do more jumping around in a night than the goddam waitresses. Before Andy saw us at the Cafe Bizarre (which isn't exactly the Copa) we were busting our balls in work. Up to here. And you can't do anything creative when you're struggling to keep the basic stuff coming. Now it seems we have time to catch our breath. We have more direction—that's where Andy comes in. We eat better, we work less, and we've found a new medium for our music. It's one thing to hustle around for odd jobs. But now we're not just another band; we're an act. See—when a band becomes an act, you get billing. You get days off. You don't just work nights—you're like, engaged."

Nightly at the Balloon Farm the Velvets demonstrate what distinguishes an act from a band. They are special. They even have a chanteuse—Nico, who is half goddess, half icicle. If you say bad things about her singing, she doesn't talk to you. If you say nice things, she doesn't talk to you either. Onstage, she is somewhat less communicative. All traces of melody depart early in her solo. The music courses into staccato beats, then slows into syrupy feedback. All this goes on until everyone is satisfied that the point has gotten across.

Oh yeah; the point! John Cale sits dreamily eyeing a Coke, pushes his hair back from his face to expose a bony nose, and observes: "You can't pin it down. It's a conglomeration of the senses. What we try to get here is a sense of total involvement."

"You mean acid?"

"Coming here on a trip is bound to make a tremendous difference. But we're here to stimulate a different kind of intoxication. The sounds, the visual stuff—all this bombarding of the senses—it can be very heady in itself, if you're geared to it."

John Cale is a classicist. His first composition was "written on a rather large piece of plywood." He studied viola and piano at the London Conservatory of Music and came to the United States as a Leonard Bernstein fellow. His sponsor was Aaron Copland. "We didn't get on very well," John says. "Copland said I couldn't play my work at Tanglewood. It was too destructive, he said. He didn't want his piano wrecked."

Cale pursued his vision with John Cage. On the viola, he would play a single note for as long as two hours. Then he met Lou Reed, and the sound that John calls "controlled distortion" was born. The Velvets, with Nico and Andy and all that light, began to construct a scene around the title "Exploding Plastic Inevitable." Their reviews reflect the ambivalence a quiet evening at the Balloon Farm can produce. Said the *Chicago Daily News*: "The flowers of evil are in full bloom." *Los Angeles* magazine compared the sound to "Berlin in the decadent thirties." Even Cher (of Sonny and Cher) was heard to mutter: "It will replace nothing except suicide."

Undaunted, the Velvets are popping eardrums and brandishing horsewhips on a nightly basis. "We want to try an electronic drum," says John. "It would produce subsonic sounds, so you could feel it even when you couldn't hear it. We'd then be able to add it to a piece of music, and it would be like underlining the beat." In cement.

Onstage, Gerard Malanga motions wildly: time for another set. John puts down his Coke and wraps a black corduroy jacket over his turtleneck. He slides his hair over his face, covering his nose again. Lou tucks his shirt in.

"Young people know where everything is at," he says. "Let 'em sing about going steady on the radio. Let 'em run their hootenannies. But it's in holes like this that the real stuff is being born. The university and the radio kill everything, but around here, it's alive. The kids know that."

The girl in the bark stockings is leaning against the stage, watching them warm up. "You can tell this is going to be a very atonal set," she says.

"Beautiful," sighs her partner, rolling his eyes. With a single humming chord, which seems to hang in the air, the Velvet Underground launches into another set. John squints against a purple spotlight. Lou shouts against a groaning amplifier. Gerard writhes languidly to one side. Sterling turns his head to sneeze. And Nico stands there, looking haunted. The noise, the lights, the flickering images—all happen. Everybody grooves.

From the balcony, Andy Warhol watches from behind his glasses. "Beautiful," he whispers. Sterling sneezes audibly but it seems to fit. "Beautiful." Gerard hands his partner a bullwhip and the girl in bark begins to sway. "Just beautiful."

—1966

CHAPTER 16

Catcher in the Haight

SAN FRANCISCO—On a winter evening, knots of anxious hippies assembled at San Francisco's Howard Presbyterian Church, overlooking the tree-lined mall called the Panhandle. Now and then the clusters parted to make way for an envoy from the feared and hated Straight Community.

The hippies were in church that night to hear a call for confrontation issued by the Diggers. Chet Helms, who runs the Family Dog (which runs the Avalon Ballroom) showed up with his dog. The Thelin brothers, who own the Psychedelic Shop and help put out the Haight community's enlightened paper, *The Oracle*, arrived beaded and beaming. Churchmen and social workers in mufti eyed each other suspiciously like rival CIA agents assigned to the same cell. And the HIP merchants (Haight Independent Proprietors) were well represented because they are committed to keeping the area's most precious commercial commodity—the resident hippies—satisfied.

The Diggers (their progenitors in Cromwellian England seized the land, tilled it, and gave the surplus to the people) had called the meeting through the city's press. Their access to media is hardly surprising. While some cities stomp their beatniks and others (like New York) ignore them, San Francisco displays its hippies like a redwood forest.

The Diggers, in existence only a few months, broke early and fast on the local "culture" wire. Their dispensing of free food in the Panhandle received wide coverage and when their storefront was busted the *Chronicle* contributed a front-page photo of loving, leaping Digger leaders—cleared of the charges against them.

It was Emmett Grogan's debut.

If the idea of the Haight is creative withdrawal, the Diggers mean hip resistance. If the New Community is seeped in day glo mysticism, the Diggers are the new realists, committed to an existential ethic of direct responsibility. They are the social workers of the Haight, but with this crucial difference: "We give without asking for performance in return. We work to provide the ultimate freedom for everyone to do his thing."

Ladling out Digger stew to the indigent and the curious is a small part of the game/role Grogan's people have chosen. The Diggers live in fear and awe of the Imminent 100,000. Grogan tells a skeptical merchant: "You been reading *Newsweek*? Man, this summer we're gonna see kids pouring in from all over the country. Freaky dropouts. Where they gonna stay; what're they gonna do?"

The Diggers offer food, shelter, and ultimately protection from what Grogan views as a hostile, murderous establishment. The Haight prides itself on being the vanguard of a new tribalism. It exists in flagrant opposition to the families back home. But no one is putting the Diggers down for their brand of in loco parentis. Because deprivation, disease, and delirium are a very real fringe of life in the hippie Oz.

At 23, Grogan makes the ideal catcher in the rye. A street kid, the product of Brooklyn's produce markets, he ran away to Europe at 15, bummed it, psyched out of the army, and joined the San Francisco Mime Troupe. When race riots erupted last summer in neighborhoods adjacent to the Haight, the Diggers were born. When police harassment failed to stop with the riots, they flourished.

The Digger ethic discourages a formal hierarchy. Sharing food and shelter has become a sharing of identities. They flood the community with periodic "papers" mimeographed on random stationery and signed simply the Communication Company. Trying to find a rank-and-file Digger brings the inevitable reply, "I don't know any."

This elusive structure fits perfectly with the cryptic style of the Haight. It messes the police mind, because local enforcers never know when a shabby "announcement" can mean a major insurrection. It gives the real Diggers the mysterioso of hip idols. And it fosters the illusion that whenever a hippie stumbles and falls there will be a Digger around to help him or her up.

Grogan's people have no premium on sanity in the hip community. But with their battle scars, their skill at hustling, and their grace, the Diggers have become cornerstones in the structure of the Haight. And with their inspired invisibility, no policeman ever knows when big brother may be watching.

So, when Grogan's people called for a confrontation, the hip community jumped and the straight Haight bristled. The charge was as usual: the cops are hassling. But this time, the Diggers had a specific accusation. An informant had revealed plans for a massive drug bust. The next day brought hasty denials from narcotics officials. (Only in San Francisco do such assurances come from the cops.) But a subsequent Digger epistle warned that "the man has been known to lie before. Indeed he's famous for it."

The effect of these rumors on the Haight remains dubious. The walls of the fortress closed, the Diggers manned the turrets, and inside the scene went on. Paranoia soon becomes as boring as anything else. The search in the Haight boils down to finding something stimulating that stays that way.

●　●　●

"I used to hang out on street corners in Queens. See, I was very tough at 13. Then I started staying with hippies. I'd smoked pot before I met them but with them I wasn't smoking to be evil; it was good, you know, just in itself.

"At 14, I ran away."

She arrived in San Francisco in time to become a Digger. Now she stands over the stove, stirring a seeping cauldron of Digger stew; celery, rice, and beef stock. Heads of lettuce lie rotting in the closet. Potatoes litter the back porch. Two immense milk tubs with the remnants of this afternoon's handout lie soaking in the bathtub.

This is a Digger kitchen, one of many. Grogan's people are a peripatetic lot. Their headquarters, the Free Frame of Reference ("Whenever you're hassled you just look through the frame and everything on the other side is free, including yourself"), had been busted. Their public hangouts were closed for the duration of the Great Bust. But even though this was a private apartment, it was filled with kids. Word gets around.

The runaway has agreed to fill you in on her people. She asks only that you don't mention her name—the anonymity thing again. She prefers to be called Miss Metesky, after George Metesky, the mad bomber. He is a Digger hero because, says the journalist Ralph Gleason: "He epitomizes the futility of joining or fighting the system." The girl is more specific: "We're all Meteskys," she explains. "We're a generation of schizophrenic mutants."

Her opinion is not gospel. The Digger ethic forbids arriving at definitions. A social worker who covers the Haight complains: "You can't pin the Diggers down to anything. Whenever you talk to one person about what someone else has said, they just grin and answer, 'That's his thing.' "

But the reluctance to conceptualize doesn't extend to action. The Diggers aim for nothing less than the creation of an independent kingdom in the Haight. Their rebellion against the straight hegemony is centered on rejecting money. Handouts on the Panhandle are only the beginning. The Diggers plan to run a bus down Haight Street. Donated sewing machines and fabric will provide the working tools for a co-op planned for the area. The Straight Theatre, opening this summer with a series of rock shows and happenings, may provide the vanguard for a hip corporation taking money from the squares and pouring it back into the community. The ultimate extension, a Digger farm on donated land in Napa or Sonoma, would fulfill the Cromwellian dream: till the land and share the surplus. The death of money applies to all these projects: everything—from clothing stores to bus lines—will be free. The owners of love boutiques must cringe at the thought of all that gratis gear. And the pushers: already the availability of stuff has driven some dealers to give Green Stamps with purchases; the Diggers' plans would drive them into Berkeley, where economic reality still prevails.

It will be interesting to watch the crucifixion when the Diggers drive the money changers from the temple. Grogan may attempt just that: he sees the Love-Haight relationship as so much useless mythology. The girl who calls herself Miss Metesky agrees. "The love thing is a shuck," she says. "The Diggers will continue to receive the casualties of the love generation."

Grouped around the table as she ladles out her stew are three runaways from the New York area, a go-go dancer from

Houston with her chihuahua, her husband with his guitar, and a freckled kid from Maine.

"Three years ago in Maine, I thought I was some weird minority," he says. "Here in California, I can do my thing." He dips into a bowl of stew with his fingers, and feeds the excess to a Digger dog—this one named Smedley. In the Haight, dogs often eat better than their masters.

In the living room, the couple from Houston have settled down. The husband wants a place to stay. Digger pads are usually well stocked with mattresses and look like one of Europe's seedier youth hostels. But, Miss Metesky explains, the pads are closed this week. The husband begins to grumble about what a shuck the Digger bit is, but finally he settles onto a mattress and begins to strum "The Times They Are a Changin' " on his guitar.

The landlord walks in, takes a look around, drinks some coffee, and splits. Miss Metesky explains: "He's a Digger."

"You want to know what we're about?" she sighs, smiling at the poised pad and pen. "A 14-year-old kid freaked out the other day. He was screaming 'Where's my hands?' He came to the Diggers to get food, which I guess represented warmth or his mother. He was shaking like a bastard. We had a room where he could go. If we expand the way we want, there would be fewer casualties around here. There would be—a place to go."

It all boils down to supply and demand. The Diggers are the closest thing the Haight has to a government. They coordinate culture. They run a travel bureau, a counseling service, a hippie grand hotel. They make and keep truces. Not long ago, a Hell's Angel was arrested. The Diggers marched a crowd of hippies to the precinct, raised bail on the spot, and sprung the offender. A tenuous alliance between the two groups resulted. The Angels run dances in San Francisco, not massacres. The Diggers are part of the reason.

"They don't have to be so mean anymore," Miss Metesky explains. "They've found people who are with them." Not long ago, she rode down Haight Street atop an Angel's hog to signal the start of a happening called "The Birth of the Haight." Five hundred hippies blew pennywhistles while their dogs barked. The cops stood aside and glared. Police resentment of the Diggers is understandable. Grogan's squad are the only real cops in the area. High or low, hip or straight, they stand between the kids and a fate worse than Meth.

So it didn't matter that the Great Bust never came off. While the hippies gathered in the basement of Howard Presbyterian Church, Digger leadership was upstairs behind closed doors, conferring with "community officials." If and when the raid does occur, three ministers are committed to open their churches to the fleeing hippies, and the local merchants are prepared to institute a civil suit against "police harassment."

Miss Metesky laughs; as a former New Yorker she understands the absurdity of those plans. But she reasons: "Can you just see us doing what we want to do, and then a bunch of old madmen in the last existing suits and ties come along and try to set things straight?"

She giggles again, and gives the pot a hefty stir.

—1967

CHAPTER 17

The Insulated Hippie Awakens

TORONTO—Yorkville Avenue ambles past three sanitized blocks of frame houses turned boutiques. Shade trees shelter a generous sidewalk from sunny glare, so no one really needs shades. The street's one rive gauche cafe is ideal for ogling. On Friday and Saturday nights, all of Talc Toronto are there, getting a weekend scene-tan. Their eyes are cemented to rows of neat black guardrails that line the street. Around these hitching posts, hippies sprawl, rap, and ogle back.

Real hippies! Native born and bred. Where they live is called Toronto's Village. Yorkville Avenue, dubbed "the Strip," is a main drag crammed with black light haberdasheries, coffee shoppes and rock clubs fanning their musical aromas into the street like pizza parlors in summer.

It is a hippie Disneyland, in plastic tribute to last month's Timestyle on the Now Generation. For in Yorkville, though the hucksters hustle and the cops harass, it all seems premeditated, like carnival. The hippies provide a heady freak show, but they are insulated from real degenerates and junkies. Unlike the Haight-Ashbury or the East Village, Yorkville is a high rent district. Many of the hippies who inhabit the area (a minority of those who actually make the scene) live five and six to a luxury room. It is a crowded life, but fairly clean. Even the air is remarkably reekless for a hippie neighborhood. Everyone talks about turning on, but you don't see much of it, and it's not easy to come by.

Finally, as if it were not hard enough to drop out along the Strip without landing in a net, Yorkville is curse-blessed with a coterie of indulgent journalists. Hippies express themselves on a wide variety of issues, certain they will read about it in the morning papers. What else is there in Toronto to frighten the gentry, with wars and riots happening elsewhere?

On a good night flashbulbs pop like strobe lights along the Strip. With media weaving among the teenyboppers, Yorkville has produced its own corps of celebrities. Robert Gilgour, a 67-year-old pensioner, is known on every city desk as "a friend to all hippies." He keeps a freezer full of sandwiches for hungry kids (though not many starve on Yorkville Avenue, with home often a suburb away) and inspires a small band of followers who call themselves '49ers.

Then there are the bikers. In Toronto, they are called the Vagabonds, and they sputter through the amiable bi-lanes on their California-style choppers. That is, occasionally! More often, you see them in small bands, colors hanging limply around their shoulders, rapping with the street hippies who worshipfully announce the presence of a "Vag" in the vicinity.

If they aren't around, a rock star or a draft dodger can make a tourist's evening out. Yorkville is thought to be filled with both. For musicians, the logo "just back from New York" is as ubiquitous as a minimum in Toronto's rock cellars. But the most mystical fixtures—the Paupers, the Mandalas, Kensington Market, or Luke and the Apostles—are not to be seen in Yorkville on summer nights. Recording and travel gigs come first and, as for leisure, the street is just too gross for a superstar.

Draft dodgers, on the other hand, are easy enough to come by in Yorkville, but difficult to authenticate. Actually, most Americans avoid the hip scene because of the ease with which they can be deported. But groupies flock to any stranger who announces his exile. It is only when the immigrant reveals his real home town (Saskatoon) in a moment of weakness that the shoulders shrug, the brows bristle in annoyance, and the backs turn utterly.

But teenyboppers are not the only ones who think Yorkville is swollen with draft dodgers. The gray populace sees the hip community as augmented and inspired by unwashed, unrepentant, un-Canadian youth. Widely published reports negate this theory, but it persists. Mothers and ministers have suggested that the hippies be driven across the border (preferably over Niagara Falls), where they will be drafted instantly. Not a few Canadians have come to the conclusion that all hippies anywhere are really Americans in disguise.

After all—hippies in Toronto? Flower children germinating among the neat cottages and Eskimo art shops? Gurus in a city where the French and Indians know their place? The Love Generation commuting to its appointed rounds on North America's cleanest subway system?

Marshall McLuhan must have brought them, much the way a filthy neighbor brings roaches, and he can take them back to New York with him, where they belong. Not a few of Toronto's gentry blame their city's philosopher-king for the hip incursion. McLuhan is more highly regarded than heeded here, and he is only incidentally an influence on the cultural mores of Toronto. Media-gazing will never replace ice hockey. Still, McLuhan's tenure has given this town a heady whiff of big-city chic. To the literati, hippies are its fruition (these days it takes a rebellious youth, not a skyline, to make a city). But to the sofa-squatters, they are its unwanted legacy. And Toronto is a midwestern matron, rising on the Great Lakes in mini-majesty. She sips her avant garde in small, sweet doses like a cocktail. Getting stoned is not allowed.

● ● ●

She stood leaning against a guardrail, surveying the Strip: Mary Kerson, the Digger from New York. A veteran of all the great wars—from Tompkins Square to Steve Paul's Scene—she had come to Toronto to help the local Diggers incorporate. There was to be a fully licensed hostel for indigent hippies, a food-distribution center, a medical clinic, and possibly a newspaper.

It made the papers. The kids on the Strip buzzed with excitement. Even the Village Bar Association (two young lawyers-in-training who staff a table on the street to check on civil liberties violations) noticed the change. Their clients weren't whimpering about illegal search and seizure anymore. They were boning up on penalties for civil disobedience.

The clarion call came from a small mascot named Dog. One tourist-ridden night he was pushed from the jammed sidewalk into the path of the cruising caravan. Dog's death brought a long-standing grievance to the fore. The kids wanted their street closed to traffic. What they were really demanding was an end to the tourist trade, and at that prospect, the owners of Yorkville balked.

So, when a small hippie band danced around a bonfire in the middle of Yorkville Avenue, six were arrested. That night, 350 of their friends sat in the street. With 3,000 onlookers whooping it up and traffic stalled for blocks, they had finally broken the rules.

The vans pulled up slowly. A force of tactical police set about cleaning up the demonstrators, while reinforcements detoured traffic onto Yorkville Avenue, so that the flow would be especially heavy. The hippies linked arms, giggling, chanting, and displaying profiles of their tongues for the press. They couldn't be pulled apart. But as bulbs flashed, traffic shrieked, and tourists jeered, the police came apart instead. Aided by squads of plainclothesmen, they waded into the jangling squatters and slammed away. It was what the Stateside hippies call a "police riot," and it seemed as though the ground rules had been laid on Sunset Strip. Screaming hippies were clubbed and pummeled before they could move. Ribs cracked, blood flowed, hair came loose. A demonstrator was hurled headfirst into a waiting van. One girl, her hand smashed under a policeman's boot, narrowly avoided having it amputated. And, as the crowd threatened to join in, a phalanx of policemen dragged the friend of all hippies—Robert Gilgour—off to jail.

That was too much. As the presses rolled, the people of Toronto learned over morning coffee that their finest had brutalized a peaceful demonstration. Amid an embarrassed insistence that only necessary force was used ("These reporters," scowled a police deskman. "In some cities, they're hard on hoods. Here, it's us."), the hippies held another sit-in, this one in the gray corridors of the old City Hall. Clerks and cops watched in stunned silence as the kids cheered whenever a prisoner was released. A stout, smiling photographer asked injured hippies to hold up their bandages for display. He snapped, beamed, and snapped again. When Gilgour was released, waving limply, the photographer nearly split his cheeks with delight.

"Hold it; hold it, pops."
He did.

• • •

When Dave De Poe joined the Company of Young Canadians (roughly equivalent to VISTA) at 23, he chose to take up residence in Yorkville. He rented a house off the Strip, went about making friends, and started the Diggers. De Poe's father, a well-known TV commentator, disapproved. The tension between them made De Poe a natural celebrity in Yorkville, but his talent for organization made him a useful one. He walked the streets like everyone's favorite worker-priest, in a flat-brimmed hat, beard, and blue jeans. With assistants like Brian (Blues) Chapman he built a tight yet casual net around the Strip, catching in the rye.

To Downtown Toronto, De Poe was regarded as an agitator—the cause, not the mitigator, of hip lawlessness. When the riots came, he was down in the street, and the police tagged him instantly as a ringleader. Only his position with the CYC kept De Poe from becoming the brunt of their frustration. As one officer raised his fist, another intervened with the riot line of the year: "Not him, for heaven's sake. He works for the federal government."

De Poe's supervisor, Alan Clarke, reported that exchange from his desk in Ottawa, where he had been asked by reporters to defend his employee against charges of agitation. Clarke said De Poe's involvement in the scene had actually been "beneficial in Yorkville." He told a reporter: "As far as we're concerned, he is where we want him to be."

On the afternoon following his second arrest, De Poe sat in his living room, welcoming visitors from one of Canada's larger television stations. The director chatted softly about his "project."

"We're doing this hippie thing, Davey. And what we plan is, we'll pick you up tomorrow, and take you out to—oh, somewhere in the suburbs, and just ask you what you think of it. You know, just stand there and tell us what you think."

De Poe, who had not slept in two days, nodded lamely, as two cameramen and a lady reporter in high tweed arrived to set up. "Let's get some of these posters in," she chortled. "who is this one—Mao?"

"Ho!" De Poe muttered, lacing up a sneaker.

"Oh don't do that just yet. Can you . . . er . . . take your shirt off and we'll just catch you putting it on? Don't put your socks on yet. . . oh, you're not going to wear socks. Oh, and . . . you're. . . uh. . . your underwear is, um, sticking out in front."

Cameras finally rolling, De Poe began his lecture. "What the pickets in the street mean is 'We'd like to talk to the people of Toronto. We want to ask the Mayor about closing our street.' But the mayor is uptight."

Blues raced up the stairs and burst into view before the cameras. "Cops are already gathering in the park." he puffed. "They're in plain clothes all over the Village."

The camera clicked shut. The reporter stepped forward, fingering a tiny rhinestone earring. "Would you say that again? We can . . . um . . . use that to set up for what's going to happen later . . . uh, potentially, of course."

● ● ●

Yorkville Avenue at dusk looked like an encampment three hours after retreat. The hippies were prepared for a rally at the nearby Queens Park love-in turf, and later that night another sit-in. This time, police estimated 5,000 tourists would clog the already strangulated strip. Even the merchants were a bit uneasy.

On the street, slings and bandages decorated in art nouveau were everywhere. Newspapers covered the sidewalks as tight clusters of hippies read about themselves and their opponents. The archvillain was controller Alan Lamport, who demanded that hippies be banished from Yorkville for a full year. "Some of them think they can get anything their sweet heart desires," he told the *Toronto Star*. "They have a spoiled brat attitude."

Dave De Poe left his house, cameramen and reporters trailing behind. Down the street, a kid with matted hair raced into an alley, pursued by a stout, crewcut plainclothesman. De Poe darted away while Blues distracted the TV crew with an imaginary scuffle up ahead. When they found him five minutes later, De Poe was heading the line of march toward Queens Park. Waving placards and incense, they made their way down tree-lined streets, while dinnertime strollers gaped.

106

On Hippie Hill, the '49ers distributed oranges and peanut butter sandwiches. Members of the Village Bar collected complaints of police brutality, preparing for a massive civilian suit. Then, with no chanting of "Hare Krishna" (that litany hasn't arrived here yet), the meeting got under way.

De Poe counseled moderation, but avoided a firm stand. From the sidelines, his father watched sullenly. It was the first time he had seen his son in action. Later, the two met briefly, and parted with their backs turned.

As lampposts flickered on across Toronto, the hippies returned to their Strip. Already, Yorkville Avenue was jammed beyond recognition with bystanders searching in vain for the real hippies. When they arrived, the police—in a far more sober mood after the morning papers—edged away from the sidewalks and waited.

But no one sat in the street that night. When a cluster of hippies fell to their knees on the sidewalk, the police moved gingerly, forcing them to stand, but not rushing them. Their orders were encased in words like "please" and "sir." Only eight arrests were made all evening, and the crowds grew restless. They tried to goad the police into action. Short haired kids from the suburbs vowed to act on their own if the hippies couldn't. The hippies found themselves outflanked by juicers; nearly half the arrests involved drunkenness.

It was a tense scene. So, word spread through the hippies' ranks: split. They moved silently back to the park, leaving the police to face a concentrated version of Yorkville on any Saturday night.

Queens Park was midnight still when the hippies arrived. They sat silently around their hill, as Dave De Poe told them he had to leave for an appearance on a late-night TV talk show. He parted with the words, "We're winning."

And they were. In three days, they had shattered their own insulation, and made a sterile stretch of plastic bohemia something worth fighting over. In Montreal and Vancouver, kids were picking up their morning papers and marveling.

Maybe next year at this time, the hippies will be stopping traffic on Yorkville Avenue with uprooted trees. Maybe Dave De Poe and Blues will collect money to send their friends to Europe. Maybe they will mix with the beautiful people and go the penthouse route. But it will be a while before Toronto society makes the Yorkville hippies an in-crowd, and perhaps they won't accept that title when it comes. They looked far better sitting in Queens Park eating oranges as a sister-Digger from New York told them: "We're a movement now, and we've got to sound like one."

Everyone agreed—they should sing "We Shall Overcome," but nobody knew the words. So Mary Kerson from the East Village led them, line by line, and they sang softly as red embers from cruising squad cars singed the trees above.

—1967

CHAPTER 18

The Long Hot Summer on Blue Jay Way

HOLLYWOOD—Laurel Canyon is a ghetto bounded by Sunset Strip and the sky. It is to California rock what the West Side is to New York's literary scene—a habitat. In its temperate sunforests live musicians, their producers, managers, gurus, and better-paid fans. The motif is au naturel, which means working fireplaces and raw wood furniture untarnished by Formica. There are no cellar scenes to make, and not a cockroach in sight to uphold avant garde tradition. The streets—with names like Robin, Oriole, and (yes) Blue Jay Way—twist among the hills like earthworms. The sun seems eternal, and it makes you ache to sever everything within that cares. It's hard to feel anxious in Laurel Canyon. You skip your mind across headlines, breadlines, and deadlines to ponder a neon butterfly disguised as a teenybopper who has just caught your eye.

But these days, a hazy fear is obscuring the sunscape in the groovy ghetto. You can hear it over coffee on the Strip. It comes with the chili at Barney's Beanery (the Max's Kansas City of the West). It confronts you at the private discotheques where Hollywood's various elites brush against each other and mutter "Pardon me, man." The Long Hot Summer. That phrase has become an American obsession, but nowhere is its utterance more startling than in Hollywood. Yet today, the sight of a thin column of smoke rising from the direction of Watts brings an anxious glance at the calendar. Every brawl and mugging is heard as an overture. Every demo looks like a Tet invasion. Though the chosen people of Laurel Canyon are not yet buying guns, their attitude is almost the equivalent of hysteria out here—that is, they are actually uptight.

"It's really going to happen. That's a little hard to believe, I know, when you've been brought up to see things in a continuum. But this is where the line ends. I'll probably go to Mexico, Canada—somewhere. But I want to see it first; I want to watch this city go down."

When they talk about the Long Hot Summer in Laurel Canyon they mean more than carnage in Watts. They are talking about the possibility of youth riots here on a scale unheard of in my lifetime. The war, the draft, and the dope laws have just about incinerated the flower child in this city. From the ashes, a militant psychedelic left has arisen. They dress even more flamboyantly than last year's hippies, but they walk tall in their beads, like fuchsia Panthers. They greet each other with two fingers raised in a V, a sign that can mean peace, love freedom, high, and, most important, solidarity. Their search for ecstasy has taken refuge within the politics of frustration. They, too, live in quiet fear of the Long Hot Summer—even more than everyone else, because unlike the radicals back East, they don't know which side they're supposed to be on.

They are commonly lumped together with the blacks, Mexicans, and Communists, into a composite image of the Threat. The dominant police attitude toward the hip community is that: they must be hit hard before they toughen up like the spades. So, when Lyndon Johnson arrived in town to attend a ceremonial dinner, police met 10,000 demonstrators along the Avenue of the Stars with unsheathed clubs. The ensuing melee—in which women, children, and cripples were singled out for savage beating—was labeled a "police riot" by the *Los Angeles Free Press*. Enforcement officials insisted, in the face of complaints from civil libertarians throughout the state, that their tactics were neither random nor sadistic but the most practical way to disperse a threatening crowd.

In effect, they asserted that what is efficient cannot be considered brutal as well. That the LAPD was exonerated is no surprise. To muzzle the police seems like heresy here, because in this city of the future a cop is one crucial link to a more paternal past. No police force in urban America functions with such freewheeling élan. The cop you are likely to meet on the Strip stands next to his bike like an erection in navy blue. His boots and shades shine; his head is enclosed in shockproof plastic white. No Hell's Angel could duplicate the swagger in his stance or the sound of his bike on an open freeway. In "peacetime," his primary purposes are to search, seize, and occasionally bust. Not just for possessing dope, but for lack of proper identification (which often comes down to a driver's license), insufficient funds, or simple "suspicion" (e.g., passing through certain neighborhoods in anything but a moving vehicle). There are also a variety of offenses involving noncooperation (the fine for using obscenity to an officer, for instance, is twice that for drunken driving on a first offense). To question arrest on such a charge is sheer masochism. In subduing a suspect, the policeman holds all the wild cards — even the joker.

"All the way down to the station, the cop in back with me, he was saying, 'You're a little whip-dick, you know that? How would you like to suck my dick?' . . . all the way down there."

That account appeared in the *Free Press* in a story about what the paper called a "copogrom" in Venice. Once the bastion of Los Angeles' beat generation, Venice today is a collection of adobe shacks, oil pumps, and muddy canals in search of a neighborhood. But its flat desolate quality, and its traditional tolerance of slumming iconoclasts, make it an ideal locale for a Haight-Ashbury of the southland. A few head shops have already opened along the peeling colonnades.

But Venice is also the site of an ambitious private renewal program. High- and low-rise luxury flats are springing up along the shallow inlets, and between the oil slicks, the Formica fingerprints of modern L.A. are already visible. This real estate boomlet is one explanation for the dragnets that have swept hip Venice recently. In the preceding week, police in plain clothes and unmarked cars made 93 arrests over their usual quota. Among the raided premises was a head shop called Earth Rose. An array of hookahs and pipes was seized under a law forbidding the possession of "narcotics paraphernalia."

Since most radicals find it impossible to separate the dominant community from its police, the psychedelic left sees the Venice busts as part of a harassment campaign against the underground. But they are afraid that come the Long Hot Summer, even such procedures will seem restrained. Paranoia strikes deep in Laurel Canyon and environs. To believe supporters of the Venice Survival Committee, California (if not America) is in the throes of a proto-fascist fit. All that is missing is the presence of a leader with the charisma to turn frustration into dogma. The polarization of the state's political life into the Wallace right and the Peace and Freedom left is one sign to them that the roots of such an upheaval are already present; that the traditional American abhorrence of extremism may not apply here much longer. And those New Left folktales about concentration camps beyond the foothills are taken for granted out here, not because there is proof that such camps are in operation, but because some of the preliminaries to actual detainment are already a reality.

"I was walking down the Strip with my girl and these cops pulled up, so I braced myself. But all they did was, they took out this camera and—click—I'm on file. That's how they're keeping busy now...getting their dossiers together." The speaker is not a professional radical. He works in the West Coast office of a major record company. But you don't need a hookah out here to proclaim your involvement in the Long Hot Summer—only long hair.

—1967

CHAPTER 19

The Head Freak Awaits a New Son

LOS ANGELES—The 3-year-old answered the door, took a cool look at the policeman standing there, raised his full blue eyes, and declared: "Fuck off, cop."

"Where's your folks, son?"

The kid brushed his white-cotton hair out of his eyes. It fell in swirling puffs down his shoulders. "Fuck off," he repeated.

So, naturally, the policeman left.

The legend is one of many traveling the Los Angeles underground, concerning a kid who went by the name of Godo. His father, one Vitautus Alphonsus Paulekas, is the chief of a tribe known vaguely as the Freaks. In the legend, Vito is part teacher, part artist, part dancer. His hands and feet are instruments of magic; his eyes are sorcerer's eyes.

Vito is not the most articulate of wizards, but he comes on booming like thunder. His eyes jolt from briar patches of wrinkles, and there's a giggle in every statement to let you know that behind the dogma is the laughing gas of experience.

His apartment, crammed below a gymnasium, has the look of a shrine. The living room is slung with webs of beads and drapery. The bedroom is small and dark, its only window is shrouded in leaded glass. The whole place resounds with canned patter from a radio turned up to compete with the bouncing medicine balls and barbells.

All over the house, on every wall, hang pictures of Godo. In the basement, where Vito teaches sculpture, work by father and son stands in a row along walls caked with clay. Godo's water colors run to bold resolute patterns. No merging shapes or colors—just simple, certain form. Vito's busts are of leering, lipless people with gaping teeth—bug-eyed monsters crying out in Los Angelic terror.

Vito's scene could double as a set for one of those fifties Hollywood exposés that took you into a beatnik pad, where chicks danced braless to bongos while some collegiate-looking cat read poetry and smoked a jade pipe. Vito comes on like a living cliché, everybody's favorite beatnik. This explains the attention he gets from filmmakers, TV producers, and editors of girlie magazines. He looks too much the rebel to be one. His familiar blend of Love-Work-Marxism actually renders him benign, and that's what we expect from artists. Vito is cast as a nut, and therefore tolerated. He has made frequent appearances on *The Joe Pyne Show* ("to establish communication with the people of Los Angeles"), where he makes an ideal sparring partner for that reactionary jock. The rumored friendship between "Iconoclast-Vito" and "Joe-the-Brute" is no coincidence; both are roles that seem too simple to be real.

So it comes as no surprise to learn of Vito's forays into exploitation. A skin magazine features a photo spread about "a name that represents nonconformity, artistic freedom, originality . . . one of the most diversified sculptors the world has ever known." Vito is featured in films like *Girl On F Street* or *Mondo Bizarro*, neither of which will make them drool at *Cahiers du Cinéma*. "Any publicity is good publicity," he reflects. "You go through this routine with naked girls, and they pan over and show your sculpture. I believe in the object itself; once they show that, they can say anything."

If there were no Vito, the LAPD would have to invent him. His peculiar fraud is what the scene has made of him. He takes his wife Sue and his tribe (a group of 35 energized kids), and hops from club to club, grooving with the city's best rock bands. To watch them dance is a revelation. There are leaps and bounds, swaying strands of hair, and bouncing, stomping feet. Sue moves like Fay Wray caught in some frenzied Kong-embrace; neck taut, shoulders erect, hair streaming free. In the center, Vito flays the smoky air and roars. It is pure, awkward energy, because when Vito dances he lets his eyes take over his body, and all that glittering blue shows.

To the cops, Vito's people are the most brazen exponents of a life-style that is somewhere between reprehensible and forbidden. By simply being themselves, the Freaks haunt straight Los Angeles. They have no penchant for destruction, but whenever the Freaks appear they inspire such loathing terror that they might as well be shouting, "Burn, baby, burn!"

Vito claims he is "the most checked-out man is this city," elaborating: "There are plainclothesmen in all my classes, and whenever we dance somewhere, the management is threatened with all kinds of injunctions." His distaste for cops goes back a long way. At 18, he spent a year and a half in a reformatory and after that, he admits, he was busted a few more times. Vito's childhood is a hazy fairy tale. He is the son of a Lithuanian sausage maker who settled in Massachusetts. "My father's fingers became shaped for stringing frankfurters," Vito recalls. "He used to walk home with sausages wrapped around his legs."

Vito's formal education encompassed four blurred years of his life. All he chooses to remember is an early love of sculpture. "I used to fool around with clay. While the other kids were busy learning to be useful citizens, I was building naked women."

His art succeeds whether or not it is valid because it is uniquely his. His dance technique needs no aesthetic; it was perfected during Vito's career as a marathon dancer. "The marathon taught me something important," he claims. "I had to place myself entirely in the possession of my partner for three hours. I carried her through the milkman's matinee and then she carried me. After six months of that kind of trust, I learned to let go completely."

Dancer, sculptor, scofflaw. He will never come of age, says the legend. His eyes will never wrinkle. It is beautiful to watch Sue and Vito play.

His son Godo was a child's child. *Life* magazine described him as "the most beautiful child in creation, with pure blond hair to his shoulders . . . pudgy little cheeks and blue eyes that are steady and make you want to weep."

In the midst of Vito's ugliest statuary stands an angelic bust of his son. It is a stylistic anomaly: no torment, no suspicion, none of the condemnation Vito feels and shows for the straight world. Just a father looking at his son.

115

"Every place he went, Godo had an intensity with every human being," says Vito. "He sized up people long before I did, and he would tell me about them. He made love to everybody."

Godo is central to the L.A. Freak mythology. He is Apollo-Jesus, golden boy, an expert drummer at 2 1/2. But Godo is dead. It happened last December, on Vito's roof. Godo encountered a rusted trap door and started to play with it. It opened and he fell in. At the hospital, the doctors called it nothing serious and let Vito see his son. Godo lay strapped and spread-eagled on a metal table. A sterile towel covered the hole in his head. His fists were pale and clenched.

Vito opened his blue eyes wider than ever as his son cried over and over, "Help me." An hour later, Godo had hemorrhaged and died. No earthquake, no fire-and-brimstone, no final revelation. Just a baby dying. Absurdity kills myths.

Recalling that day, Vito hardens, straightens, narrows. His wrinkled lids blink shut. "The D.A.'s office is trying to get something on me for this," he insists. "I heard from people in their office that they tried to find evidence of drugs on Godo. It wasn't a rotten trap door they were after; that's legal. But drugs . . . ."

No one has to accuse Vito; the subject of responsibility comes up by itself. Why wasn't a tracheotomy performed at the hospital? Why did they tie Godo down to a table? Why was the door left to rot?

"An old friend of mine came to see us afterward," Vito recalls. "She said: 'Vito, your baby is dead. God punished you for doing the things you did with him.' " Vito's laugh becomes a nervous giggle. "My son was killed by a bum trap door, not by any God," he insists. No one accuses, but Vito feels weight on his shoulders anyway. The head Freak of Los Angeles, the ultimate iconoclast, has his own superstition: God is punishing him for immeasurable evil. Godo is dead and God, in the form of a cop, isn't through with Vito yet.

But myths never die; they only transmigrate. For a time, Godo held the legend together. He was living proof: the second Freaky generation. So the underground awaits his resurrection, and the occasion may not be far away. Sue is six months pregnant, and sewing clothes. A box of lacy nightshirts waits in anticipation.

"My baby is dancing already in Sue's belly," Vito exalts. "Sue was dancing right in this kitchen while she was in labor. When Godo was born he came out with his mouth already open, making noise."

The living legend has a new inspiration. A child messiah will be born among the Freaks. Lightning will strike Beverly Hills. Thunderbolts will shatter over Sacramento. Sunset Strip will hiss, crack, and split. Chief Vito's sorcerer's eyes will twinkle as—amid the stucco ruins—Godo is risen.

—1967

CHAPTER 20

A Groovy Idea While He Lasted

NEW YORK—We are all victims of symbols. Events breed their own ritual. Maybe that is why the murders of James Leroy Hutchinson and Linda Fitzpatrick read like act three of an off-off-Broadway play. The truest theater of the sixties lies spiked across the city desk, slugged "slay."

What happened at 169 Avenue B happens all the time. A man and woman are hauled or lured down to the boiler room, where, amid rags and rat-smell she is raped and both are stomped dead.

Such crimes become incidents. We never hear about them unless the woman was white, pregnant, or mutilated. But Groovy and his girl were slaughtered right on page one of the *Daily News*. Journalists made pilgrimages to Tompkins Square and its adjoining shrines. Even Mayor Lindsay took note. When he called the murders "a tragedy," he was speaking not about the crime but its particulars. The tragedy in what went down on Avenue B is who went down, and who did the felling.

Some crimes seem to crystallize an age. This time, only the corpses make it improper to write off victims and villains as an allegory staged by some playwright-deity. We would have waited in line to see it in the theater, specifying alternate dates, while on a stage set as a boiler room, hippies and black militants dance a stylized ballet.

Photos were plentiful. "His own weird world turned against him," crooned the *Daily News*. Centerfold obituaries immortalized Groovy as a speed-saint, guru-clown, lover-dealer.

119

How well he personified his love ethic, and how much more perfect he was as a symbol than he must have been as a man.

He and his girl were buried last week in their respective cultures. Linda's velvet-draped casket was carried down an Episcopal aisle while the minister chanted from the Book of Common Prayer. She rode to her burial in a gray Cadillac. Groovy's funeral was conducted in a Baptist minister's parlor. As a eulogy, Galahad played the harmonica that was part of his friend's costume.

Neither coffin was notably arrayed with flowers, which was appropriate. Both were victims of such symbolism. They were beautiful people, and beautiful victims. They followed their supposed assailants into the basement, exuding love and groove. And they died near a pile of their clothing, not merely rubbed out but smashed faceless.

The News eulogized Linda Fitzpatrick as "a pretty fair-skinned aspiring artist who clung to the fringes of hippiedom, terrified of the denizens of that accursed land, but fascinated by them." Gone are Linda's beads and bangles; the papers were filled with rich-girl snapshots. She too lost her personality to allegory. Her swirling stares and speed-chatter were buried in a polished coffin. To the News and its audience, she was not high but afraid.

That fear is all over the East Village today. The murders were too plausible to be ignored, the suspects too familiar to be dismissed. No one escapes the media, including its antagonists. Everyone knows that Groovy died in a pool of his own blood. And suddenly, other killings come to mind; not the publicized ones—like the fatal stabbing of Walter Coey on his stoop on East 11th—or the bizarre ones—like the Central Park mugging of Bruce Mante, "the poet," and the rape of his 15-year-old "flower bride." They remember the casual murders (five or six since the early summer, some claim). Accounts of unreported rape abound, and hallway muggings seem to be a rite of passage east of Tompkins Square.

It is a slum; Groovy's death reminds us of that. And hippies, they mutter, are the new niggers. "Flower power was a summer vacation," one hippie hisses. "In San Francisco, they staged the death of the hippie. Here, we got the real thing."

The mindblower is not that love is dead in the East Village, but that it has taken this long to kick the bucket. Flower power began and ended as a cruel joke. The last laugh belongs to the mediamen, who chose to report a charade as a movement. In doing so, they created one. By the thousands, the real victims of flower hype poured into the slums of both coasts. *LifeLook* filled its pages with technicolor testimonials to the young drop-outs living the love ethic their leaders were wary of. The hippies tried to warn their suburban following through the under-ground press, but the copy poured thin, like Digger stew. Through it all was a bizarre camaraderie between the fourth estate and the fifth dimension. Every paper picked its own hippie spokesman. The *Post* latched onto Abbie Hoffman, and in their tradition of prophetic misprints, called his followers "Happies." The *Times* found Galahad, and made him the East Village Lawrence of Arabia. Reluctant, willing, or both, these men, too, became symbols. Those who accepted their pronouncements became victims.

The flower children brought their material feast to areas of constant famine, and then went on a hunger strike. Even in rags, they seemed wealthy. Even destitute, they knew their rights and privileges. The attention they won from the press and the police made reprisals inevitable. "The hippies really bug us," a young black East Sider told the *Times*. "Because we know they can come down here and play their games for a while and then escape. And we can't, man."

Only now, after Groovy's murder, is there talk about the madness of counseling large-scale settlement of the ghetto by dropouts from the middle class. Only now are flower children wondering why anyone would sleep in Central Park, or offer flowers to a raging madman. And only as the Summer of Love yields a violent harvest is there talk of getting out. Like generations of Lower East Siders before them, the Group Image wants to move to the country. Abbie Hoffman wants to split for San Francisco. In supermarkets and psychedelic shops, a rash of neatly printed notices has appeared, offering cash for the return of a son or daughter. The old folks are scared, but so are their kids.

Groovy's legacy is a new slum-hippie, who lives in the ghetto and acts like it. He sees the scene for what it is. "The mystique has worn off," he says. "People are beginning to admit the ugliness of it now. The myths are peeling away, like bad paint, man. Take the drug thing. This is an amphetamine scene here. Part of your flower power survival kit is Meth. It's ugly, and it's real, man. And it was here all along, for anyone to see who felt like it."

New hippie is on the scene. Galahad helped usher him in when he told the *News*: "Just give me ten minutes alone with whoever did this to my friend Groovy." The word has gotten around that some Diggers in New York and San Francisco carry guns—and intend to use them. The flower child, not a veteran of violence, is toughening up.

"I respect those who respect me," he says, with a passing glance at the east side of Tompkins Square Park. You ask about the mood on the streets, and from beneath his robes, he produces a wooden shaft painted in Day Glo swirls. It snaps open to reveal an erect steel blade.

—1967

PART III

The Madness

CHAPTER 21

Theater of Cruelty: King in Chicago

CHICAGO—Hit squarely between the shoulder blades, Reverend Martin Luther King closed his eyes and fell to one knee. He waited for the impact of the bullet. But King had been struck by a rock. He brushed off the back of his neck, told reporters he was fine, and signaled his followers on.

They followed. More than 800 strong, they walked two abreast through Chicago's Gage Park area last Friday, led by officials of King's Southern Christian Leadership Conference. Twelve hundred policemen tried to prevent the march from becoming a bloodbath. The demonstrators inched their way through a hail of bricks, bottles, firecrackers, and spit while 7,000 white residents of the area screamed abuse.

Chicago is a poor place to demonstrate the validity of nonviolence. This year's quota of race warfare was far more vicious here than anywhere in the nation. The city's Roman Catholics are scattered in tight ethnic enclaves; they're neither rich enough to tolerate newcomers nor organized enough to meet the civil rights revolution with anything more destructive than bricks and cherry bombs.

The black power schism has created a profound enmity among the lower echelons of Chicago's black leadership. One militant leader, who wore a Black Panther insignia as he spoke, called the SCLC march "King's last stand." He was a bit unkind. But many accept his premise—that King's 35-point program to "make Chicago an open city" is, in part, an effort to wrest control from the militants of the place they now hold in the hearts and headlines of America.

125

Chicago's newspapers are filled with hair-raising stories about vast black gangs on the South Side. Tales of the Mighty Blackstone Rangers, which the *Chicago Daily News* calls "the biggest, toughest, and best disciplined gang Chicago has produced in a decade," are filling the copy gap between the last mass murder and the next tax hike. All of which makes this town one hell of a place to stage a comeback. But that's what SCLC's ambitious program amounts to. It calls for more public housing construction in racially mixed areas, the establishment of a bargaining union for welfare recipients, and a civilian review board. It's too early to tell whether the program or the marches will succeed. But Martin Luther King and his followers proved one thing last Friday: they showed Chicago and the nation that the southerner is everyman.

King appeared first for the TV cameras. He stood on the steps of the Friendship Missionary Baptist Church on West 71st Street, while demonstrators piled into cars and headed west, past the wooden fire escapes and backyard alleys that spell slum in Chicago. Suddenly, across a thoroughfare called Normal Boulevard, everything became hostile and white. Clusters of onlookers booed from the sidewalks at the passing motorcade. Neighborhood kids on bicycles rode alongside, pointing and spitting.

The cars deposited demonstrators and reporters in Marquette Park. After the previous Sunday's march, gangs of whites had roamed through this area setting fire to demonstrators' cars. This time, cars and drivers returned to the black quarter, leaving hundreds of tense marchers camped along the grassy slopes, waiting for things to start. They didn't wait long. Gangs of white youths tossed stones and sticks from across a narrow river. A brawl broke out in the parking area. And passing cars honked in protest. The police arrived in chartered city buses and quickly cleared the area. Blue shock helmets bobbed among the weeping willows and along the paths where King would walk. There had been rumors of land mines.

"I hope King gets it," said a neighborhood boy named John, waving a Confederate flag in the direction of the marchers. "We was chased twice and we ain't gonna move again." A friend held a sign that said "Wallace for President." "I'll go to school with 'em and I'll work with 'em," he said, "but I won't live with 'em.

I seen what they done to their neighborhoods and I don't want 'em doing it here."

Gage Park is a Polish-Lithuanian ghetto. Many of its residents moved there from other neighborhoods where Catholic churches have since become Baptist or Pentecostal. They stand on their porches awaiting the nigger invasion. The anger of genuine frustration is on their faces. They hold their children and scream "White power!" and "Get that priest out of there; he's no priest." But over the insults and the clenched fists, they tell you: "We won't move again."

The line moved slowly through the park. Two brown banners at the head proclaimed the movement's insignia: a V encased in a circle. Veteran demonstrators began to sing, but the marshals ordered quiet. Over the silence were the sounds of shuffling feet, the crack of nightsticks against policemen's thighs, and the distant roar of car horns.

On California Avenue, the crowd marched past rows of neat porches and shrubbery. "Keep your slums; we don't want 'em," one mother screamed. "Kill coon King," chanted a group of old men. And two teenagers who said they were "some of the boys from Saint Rita's" warned: "It's gettin' dark soon; then there'll be some action."

King, in a gray suit, blue shirt, and no tie, was almost hidden from sight by his followers. Whenever the group stopped, they covered his head with picket signs. The sidewalks were filled with shouting, spitting whites. Firecrackers exploded freely among the marchers. Those hit limped on. A priest picked up a brick that had hit him in the shoulder and put it in his pocket. A knife, thrown at King, hit a young student instead; police carried him away as the crowd roared its approval. When the entire march halted before the Mark Realty Company, which has allegedly refused to serve black applicants, the street exploded with boos and cries of "We want [George Lincoln] Rockwell." A silent prayer was pockmarked by breaking bottles and exploding cherry bombs that the crowd lobbed into the kneeling demonstrators.

When the marchers returned to Marquette Park to disperse, they were followed by a mob estimated at 5,000 whites. Hecklers lined a slope, cheering whenever a firecracker exploded, like fans at a football game. Clouds of dust covered the area as police chased charging youths through the grass. One man kicked a policeman in the leg and received a sharp blow across the face. Blood oozed from his nostrils and forehead; he began to cry. Three policemen pinned his hands and carried him away. A youth was tossed into a paddy wagon, his shirt splashed with blood. An injured policeman writhed on the ground while four more cops felled his assailant and applied handcuffs. Teenagers began to scale a high fence to reach the marchers, but police knocked them down with flailing billy clubs.

Amid the screaming mob, 800 marchers huddled in the roadway waiting to be piled into police buses. Lewis Cole, a young New Yorker who is in Chicago for the summer to work with SCLC, blamed the Catholic educational system for the riot. "These folks actually believe Negroes have tails." Cole, who has traveled through the South, is a firm believer in nonviolence. "You don't beat a crazy man, he said. "You take him to the psychiatrist." Suddenly a cherry bomb exploded at Cole's feet. He grabbed his knee and rolled over in pain as a small crowd of women squealed with delight.

"I still love 'em," he said.

Busload after busload of marchers pulled out of the area. Police swinging nightsticks charged a pack of teenagers blocking the roadway, but they left the thousands on the slope alone. "If that crowd breaks through," one cop said, "it's gonna be the end."

On one bus, the marshal ordered all windows closed. The vehicle pulled away amid a hail of spit. No longer protected by the police, it sped through the hostile white streets. Stones and bottles flew from the sidewalks. The marshal shouted, "Everyone duck." A window shattered and one marcher picked up a huge yellow brick that had hit him in the head. His scalp bled from three places. A second window cracked and glass spilled freely over the rear section.

Once across Normal Boulevard the marshal shouted: "We made it." The bus rang with cheers and freedom songs. From the porches, ladies smiled. From small shops, merchants and customers waved. From the sidewalks, young toughs clapped and sang along. Suddenly, no one was screaming "Burn, baby, burn" and there were no Molotov cocktails hidden in the alleys. It was like the good old days, before nonviolence became passé.

Martin Luther King, Nobel Prize winner, pacifist, agitator, leader, and ex-leader, had faced 5,000 white Chicagoans who wanted to see his throat slit. He told those few reporters who had not left for cover: "I've never seen so much hostility in a demonstration before. And I've been all over the South."

A flying brick screamed, "Amen."

—1966

CHAPTER 22

Theater of the Absurd: Insurrection at Columbia

Fold

NEW YORK—You could tell something was brewing at Columbia University by the crowds around the local Chock Full, jumping and gesturing with more than coffee in their veins. You could sense insurrection in the eyes peering from windows where they didn't belong. And you knew it was revolution, for sure, from the trash.

Don't underestimate the relationship between litter and liberty at Columbia. Until last Tuesday, the university was a clean dorm, where students paid rent, kept the house rules, and took exams. Then the rebels arrived, in an uneasy coalition of hip, black, and leftist militants. They ransacked files, shoved furniture around, plastered walls with paint and placards. They scrawled on blackboards and doodled on desks. They raided the administration's offices where they claim to have found cigars, sherry, and a dirty book.

The rebels totaled upward of 900 during peak hours. They were ensconced behind sofa-barricades. You entered Fayerweather Hall through a ground-floor window. Inside, you saw blackboards filled with "strike bulletins," a kitchen stocked with sandwiches and cauldrons of spaghetti, and a lounge filled with squatters. There was some pot and a little petting in the corridors. But on Friday, the rebellion had the air of a college bar at 2:00 a.m. In nearby Avery Hall, the top two floors were occupied by architecture students, who sat at their drawing boards creating plans for a humanistic city and taping their finished designs across the windows. In Low Library, the strike steering committee occupied the offices of President Grayson Kirk. On the other side of the campus, the mathematics building was seized late Friday afternoon. The rebels set about festooning walls and making sandwiches. Jimi Hendrix blared from a phonograph. It was a most eclectic uprising, and a most forensic one as well. The debates on and around the campus were endless. Outside Ferris Booth Hall, two policemen in high boots took on a phalanx of SDS supporters. Near Low Library, a radical in a lumberjack shirt met a frat man in a London Fog. "You've got to keep your people away from here. We don't want any violence," said lefty. "We have been using the utmost restraint," answered his adversary. "But," insisted the lumberjack shirt, letting his round glasses slide down his nose, "this gentleman here says he was shoved."

In its early stages, at least, it was a convivial affair, a spring carnival without a queen. One student climbed a tree outside Hamilton Hall and shouted for all to hear: "This is a liberated tree. And I won't come down until my demands have been met."

Spindle

Rap Brown stood in the lobby of Hamilton Hall, reading a statement to the press. His followers stood around him, black and angry. It was 7:30 p.m. Sunday, and the press had been escorted across a barricade of tabletops to stand in the lobby while Brown read his group's demands. By now, there were dozens of committees and coalitions on the campus, and students could choose from five colors of arm bands to express their sympathies: red indicated pro-strike militancy, green meant peace with amnesty, pale blue meant an end to demonstrations, white stood for faculty, and black indicated support for force.

But no faction worried Columbia's administrators more than the blacks. They had become a political entity at 5:00 a.m. Wednesday morning when 300 white radicals filed dutifully from Hamilton Hall at the request of the blacks. From that moment, the deserted building became Malcolm X University, identified by a sign over the main door. In the lobby were two huge posters of Stokely Carmichael and Malcolm X. That was all whites were allowed to see of Hamilton Hall. The blacks insisted on holding out alone, but by joining the demands of the people in Harlem and the kids in Low, they added immeasurable power to the student coalition. To expel the students from Hamilton meant risking charges of racism, and that meant turning Morningside Park into a rather vulnerable DMZ. To eject only the whites would leave the University with the blame for arbitrarily deciding who was to be clubbed and who spared.

In short, the blacks made the administration think twice. And Rap Brown knew it. He read his statement to the press, and after it was over, looked down at those of us taking notes and muttered, "Clear the hall." We left.

There was a second factor in the stalemate. The issue of university control raised by the radicals had stirred some of the more vocal faculty members into action. They arrived in force on Friday night, when it became known that police were preparing to move. When the administration issued a one-hour ultimatum to the strikers early Saturday morning, concerned faculty members formed an ad hoc committee and placed themselves between the students and the police. This line was defied only once—at 3:00 a.m. Saturday by two dozen plainclothesmen. A young French instructor was led away with a bleeding head. The administration backed down, licked its wounds, and waited. It played for time, and allowed the more militant faculty members to expend their energies on futile negotiations. All weekend, the campus radio station, WKCR, broadcast offers for settlement and their eventual rejection. While the Board of Trustees voted to suspend construction of the gymnasium pending further study, they made it clear that their decision was taken at the mayor's request, and that they were not acceding to any of the strikers' demands. Over the weekend, factions multiplied and confusion grew on campus. This too played into the administration's hands. When a line of conservative students formed around Low Library to prevent food from being brought to the protesters, the administration ordered food for the anti-picket line at the school's expense.

Finally, the first formal faculty meeting in anyone's memory was called for Sunday morning. But only assistant, associate, and full professors were present. With this qualification, the administration assured itself a resolution that would seem to signify faculty support. Alone and unofficial, the ad hoc committee persisted in its demands, never quite grasping its impotence until late Monday night, when word began to reach the campus that the cops would move.

Mutilate

At 2:30 Tuesday morning, policemen poured onto the campus. The students were warned of the impending assault when the University cut off telephone lines in all occupied buildings. One by one, the liberated houses voted to respond nonviolently.

While plainclothesmen were being transported up Amsterdam Avenue in city buses marked "special," a uniformed force moved first on Hamilton Hall. The students there marched quietly from their sanctuary after police reached them via the school's tunnels. There were no visible injuries as they boarded a bus to be led away, and this tranquil surrender spurred rumors that a mutual cooperation pact of sorts had been negotiated between police and black demonstrators.

Things were certainly different in the other buildings. Outside Low Memorial Library, police rushed a crowd of students, clubbing some with blackjacks and pulling others by the hair. Uniformed police were soon joined by plainclothesmen, identifiable only by the tiny orange buttons in their lapels. Many were dressed to resemble students. Some carried books, others wore Coptic crosses around their necks. You couldn't tell, until they started to operate, that they were cops.

At Mathematics Hall, police broke through the ground-floor windows and smashed the barricade at the front door. Students who agreed to surrender peacefully were allowed to do so with little interference. They walked between rows of police, through Low Plaza, and into vans that lined College Walk. In the glare of floodlights, the prisoners waved their hands in victory signs and sang "We Shall Overcome." A large crowd of sympathizers was separated from the prisoners by a line of police, but their chants rocked the campus. Police estimated that at least 628 students were jailed. Officials at nearby Saint Luke's Hospital reported that 74 students were admitted for treatment. This figure did not include those who were more seriously injured, since they were removed to Knickerbocker Hospital by ambulance. Three faculty members were reportedly hurt.

Many of the injuries occurred among those students who refused to leave the buildings. Police entered Fayerweather and Mathematics Halls and dragged limp students down the stairs. The sound of thumping bodies was plainly audible at times (demonstrators had waxed the floors to hamper police). Many emerged in masks of vaseline, applied to ward off the effects of Mace. Police made no attempt to gas the demonstrators. But they pummeled and kicked limp demonstrators, often with quick jabs in the stomach. I saw students pulled by the hair, scraped against broken glass, and, when they proved difficult to carry, beaten repeatedly. Outside Mathematics Hall, a male student in a leather jacket was thrown to the ground when he refused to walk and beaten by half a dozen officers while plainclothesmen kept reporters at a distance. When he was finally led away, his jacket and shirt had been ripped from his back.

The lounge at Philosophy Hall, which had been used by the ad hoc faculty committee as an informal senate, became a field hospital. Badly injured students lay on beds and sofas while stunned faculty members passed coffee, took statements, and supplied bandages. The most violent incidents had occurred nearby, in Fayerweather Hall, where many students who refused to leave were dragged away bleeding from the face and scalp. Medical aides who had moved the injured to a nearby lawn trailed the police searching for bleeding heads. "Don't take him, he's bleeding," you heard them shout. Or "Pick her up, stop dragging her."

The cries of the injured echoed off the surrounding buildings and the small quad looked like a battlefield. Though two of Mayor Lindsay's top aides, Sid Davidoff and Barry Gottehrer, had been present throughout the night, neither was seen to make any restraining move toward the police. Commissioner Leary congratulated his men. And University

135

President Grayson Kirk regretted that even such minimal violence was necessary.

By dawn, the rebellion had ended. Police cleared the campus of remaining protesters by charging, nightsticks swinging, into a large crowd that had gathered around the sundial. Now, the cops stood in a vast line across Low Library Plaza. Their boots and helmets gleamed in the floodlights. Later in the morning, a reporter from WKCR would encounter some of these arresting officers at the Tombs, where the prisoners were being held. He would hear them singing "We Shall Overcome," and shouting, "Victory!"

At present, it is difficult to measure the effect police intervention will have on the university. Most students are too stunned to consider the future. On Tuesday morning they stood in small knots along Broadway, stepping around the horse manure and watching the remaining policemen leave. Their campus lay scarred and littered. Walks were inundated with broken glass, blankets, and even discarded shoes. Flowerbeds had been trampled and hedges mowed down in some places. Windows were broken in at least three buildings and whole classrooms had been demolished.

It would take a while to make Columbia beautiful again. On that, most students agreed. And some insisted that it would take much longer before the university would seem a plausible place to teach or study in again. The revolution had begun and ended in trash, and that litter would persist to haunt Columbia.

—1968

CHAPTER 23

Theater of Fear: One on the Aisle

CHICAGO—I brought the fear out with me from New York, in a white plastic helmet and a jar of Vaseline—the same fear that built the fences, and erected the barricades, and brought all those soldiers in from Texas; the kind that burns when you tap its roots.

If you want to experience the ecstasy of street-turmoil, you must first understand the reality of fear. Because no one could have come to Chicago without first fighting in his head the battle he would later fight in the streets.

I made lists. Weeks before my first whiff of tear gas, I spent a night dissecting my motives and expectations in two neat columns. On one side, I wrote: adventure, good copy, and historical imperative. On the other: danger, loneliness, and cost. The word commitment didn't appear on either side. Not since college had I been able to associate that word with politics. I simply redirected my radicalism toward aesthetics. I never saw the stirring of revolution at Columbia, and while I agreed with their goals, I felt distinct from the student radicals and their style. My cynic's streak flowed river-deep when I witnessed the martyrdom of Mimi (one of two girls who served short terms in the Women's House of Detention and inspired the chant, "Free Huey . . . Free Mimi"). If we couldn't take punishment, did we really deserve to be free?

Not long after that, I had lunch with a Broadway producer who wanted me to help write the script for a protest-musical.

Eyes aglow, he related his opening scene. Thirty kids march onstage, carrying signs. A voice screams: "Up against the wall," and the ensemble breaks into a chorus of "We Protest," to the tune of the 1812 Overture. There has been an undeclared alliance in my mind between that scenario and the tweedy revolutionaries at Columbia. Before Chicago, I couldn't perceive the difference between guerrilla theater on Morningside Heights and the realpolitik of Broadway.

• • •

"You afraid?" I asked a kid from California. He zipped his army jacket up to his neck, and filled his palm with a wad of Vaseline. "I dunno," he answered. "My toes feel cold, but my ears are burning."

We were standing together in Lincoln Park, not long after curfew on Tuesday night, watching an unbroken line of police. Around us were 1,000 insurgents: hippies, Marxists, tourists, reporters, Panthers, Angels, and a phalanx of concerned ministers, gathered around a 12-foot cross. Occasionally a cluster of kids would break away from the rally to watch the formation in the distance. They spoke quietly, rubbing cream on their faces and knotting dampened undershirts around their mouths. Not all their accoutrements were defensive. I saw saps and smoke bombs, steel-tipped boots and fistfuls of tacks. My friend pulled out a small canister from his pocket. "Liquid pepper," he explained.

Watching these kids gather sticks and stones, I realized how far we have come from that mythical summer when everyone dropped acid, sat under a tree, and communed. If there were any flower children left in America, they had heeded the underground press and stayed home. Those who came fully anticipated confrontation; there were few virgins to violence in the crowd tonight. Most had seen—if not shed—blood.

The cops advanced at 12:40 a.m., behind two massive floodlight trucks. They also had the fear; you could see it in their eyes (wide and wet) and their mouths. All week, you watched them cruise the city, never alone and never unarmed. At night, you heard their sirens in the streets, and all day, their helicopters in the sky. On duty, the average Chicago cop was a walking arsenal with a shotgun in one hand, a riot baton (long and heavy with a steel tip) in the other, and an assortment of pistols, nightsticks, and ominous canisters in his belt. Then you saw under the helmets, and the phallic weaponry, and you felt the fear again. Immigrant to stranger, cop to civilian, old man to kid. The fear that brought the people of Chicago out into the streets during Martin Luther King's open housing march, now reflected in the fists of these cops. The fear that made the people of Gage Park spit at priests, and throw stones at nuns, now authorized to kill. And you realized that the cops weren't putting on that display for you; no—a cop's gun is his security blanket, just as Vaseline was yours.

Then the lights shone brilliant orange and the tear gas guns exploded putt-putt-puttutt, and the ministers dipped their cross into a hale of smothering fog. The gas hit like a great wall of pepper and you ran coughing into the streets, where you knew there would be rocks to throw and windows to smash and something to feel besides fear.

● ● ●

The soldiers stood on all the bridges, sealing off Grant Park from the city streets. The kids couldn't be gassed anymore, because the wind was blowing fumes across the guarded bridges and into every open pore of the Conrad Hilton, and the hotel was filled with good people who had tears in their eyes. So the soldiers just stood with their empty guns poised against the tide. And they were frowning at the kids who shouted, "Put down your guns; join us." A few hid flowers in their uniforms, and some smiled, but mostly, they stood posing for their own death masks.

"Wouldn't you rather hold a girl than a gun?" asked one kid with his arm around two willing chicks.

"You don't understand," the soldier stammered, moving his tongue across his lips. "It's orders. We have to be here."

That was Wednesday—nomination day—and the city was braced for escalation. At the afternoon rally, an American flag was hauled down, and the police responded by wading into the center of the crowd with clubs flying. The kids built barricades of vacated benches, and pelted the police with branches and plastic bags of cow's blood.

I stood in the shade applying Vaseline. I had my route mapped out in advance; across the northmost bridge and into the Loop. With every semblance of press identification I owned pinned to my shirt, I set out across the mall. But most of the crowd had the same idea. Across on Michigan Avenue, I could hear the shouts of demonstrators who were regrouping at the Hilton. I stopped to wet my undershirt in a fountain and ran down the street. My body was committed but my head remained aloof.

It brought me back to the Columbia uprising, because I learned something then about why I am a journalist, and it has stayed with me since. Near Fayerweather Hall, I came face to face with a bloodied liberator. He looked up at the press card on my jacket, and muttered: "That keeps you safe, huh?"

He was right. I demand that distance; it's part of my psyche. And I wasn't yet prepared to smash the tape recorder in my brain that retains impressions without actually experiencing them. For me, the Chicago fear amounted to going up against the wall without the little card that reads, "Police Please Pass."

But now, I found myself swept up in the crowd around the Hilton. Rolls of toilet paper fell from the windows above. Floodlights flashed, cameras snapped, and somewhere a glass pane shattered. That was enough. The cops turned on the crowd and shoved us against the hotel wall. People shrieked with one breath and apologized for stepping on toes with the next. Then the cops rushed in two directions and I fell on someone's back. A window broke behind me and I saw people falling into the hotel pharmacy. Ahead, the police were clubbing in wide circles. Up close and frozen into place, I saw their fists move in slow motion. I looked up at a kid whose arms were twisted behind in the crush, and I felt the Guernica in his eyes; the same expression on the big horse was on his lips. And I knew where it had come from and why.

I slipped out and walked across the street, shaking. I sat for 10 minutes with a girl who had been unconscious. We watched the medical crews covering their faces. And when the tear gas came, we ran away. On Michigan Avenue, I sat in the street, and ripped away the remnants of my press cards. I whooped the way they did in *The Battle of Algiers*, and chanted the way they did in *La Chinoise*, and I raised my hands in a television "V" at the flag they had lowered to half mast.

When the sirens came closer, I ran by rote up the steps of the Art Institute.

You blew your cool, I thought, but it was like watching someone else's headache. I had found the other side of fear, which is not heroism but rage. My eyes burned with it and my hands shook with it. Behind me, a cop fired over my head, and I ran forward shouting, "Pigs eat shit," not so he could hear, but so I could. In the street, I saw a straight kid in a crewneck sweater heave a rock through the window of a police car. "The first one's hard," he said, as we ran toward State Street, "but after that, it's easy."

Which is where it's at, with America and me.

—1968

CHAPTER 24

Homecoming

NEW YORK—I came back from Chicago swimming in revolution. Radicalized, I wore my face phlegmatic, like Chairman Mao. I sniffed the fall air for insurrection, and learned to invoke the proper slogans and flash the right salute. Ho, ho, ho chi minh. Whoever you say, is gonna win.

This is the most terrifying year anyone my age has had to endure. We still haven't come to terms with the public extinction of our heroes or the elevation of bureaucrats. To stand against the numbing tide of recent events requires firm roots. And we are all laying down those roots right now, by molding ourselves into a smug middle, enraged right, or determined left. It's a good time to bury your head in dogma, to gird your loins in slogans, to lose yourself in the folds of that great beast slinking toward November to be born.

This polarization is bound to have an effect on pop culture. Already the innovative frenzy of the mid (mod) sixties has become a predictable, rather sedate elaboration of existing forms. The most moving recent albums (the Byrds' *Sweetheart of the Rodeo* and the Band's *Sounds from Big Pink*) are canny evocations of traditional forms. But this season has produced no music that expresses a shattering personal vision. Our Beatles, with their ears pressed tightly to the trans-Atlantic ground, have given us a lush, effusive ballad to suckle on. I like "Hey, Jude" for its hypnotic calm, and the message of "Revolution" doesn't turn me off as much as its uninspired hard-rock shell. But both songs are explicit reflections of psychic constraint. It's as though the entire rock establishment were pulling back to reassess itself. What must eventually suffer in this tightening of reins is the precious spontaneity that characterized the pop explosion. The decadence of art rock is not its content, but its inability to transcend the rigidities of form. That's why the Doors have begun to creak and the Cream to curdle.

As America congeals into opposing masses, and the freedom to move among ideas becomes subservient to the necessity of commitment, pop culture will function as a clenched fist. Already, the liaison between the underground and the middle-brow (which produced the most widely felt pop renaissance since the twenties) is beginning to fall apart. These forgotten people, who are going to elect the next president, will soon dominate mass-culture as well. The underground will respond to this seizure by retreating into the protective isolation it cultivated during the fifties. If our choice in heroes this year is limited to George Wallace and Mark Rudd (who are both authoritarian bastards, when you think about it), our choice in art may soon amount to American Gothic or the Guernica, with no room for any vision in between.

When that happens, this column will probably cease to appear, not in any protest on my part, but because pop will no longer excite me. How long since a rock song blew your mind?

—1968

CHAPTER 25

Chapter copy

C. J. Fish on Saturday

NEW YORK—It was Saturday afternoon and the Algonquin Hotel smelled of old marble and mahogany. In his suite, Country Joe MacDonald sat on a sofa and watched cartoons on color TV. They were strange, frenzied fantasies filled with ultraviolet dragons and heroic white whales. Aggression was the dominant theme and the plots amounted to a series of battles, with flashes of color the only sign of impact. Joe watched for 20 minutes, holding a windup policeman doll in his hand. You turn the key and the head bobs and the club moves up and down.

I had come to rap about the revolution. Since the Fish have come to represent the essence of commitment in a rock group, I was searching for a reminiscence of life at the barricades, and perhaps a prediction or two. But Country Joe snickered. "There isn't going to be any revolution. Let's be realistic," he said, and went off to brush his teeth.

Barry Melton, who plays guitar and has hair like a liberated sheep, took up the TV watch. I asked him about Chicago, and what it meant to him. "Well, we were walking into this hotel, and these guys with arm bands on came by. They followed us into the lobby and attacked us." End of manifesto.

Country Joe returned wearing a brocade vest and a straw hat. He picked up the toy cop again, while Barry called room service for breakfast. "Why isn't there going to be a revolution?" I asked.

"Because you have to control things, and most of the people I know aren't ready for that. They want a leaderless society."

"What about the guerrillas?"

"I don't know any. I know a lot of people wearing Che Guevara T-shirts . . . what a bunch of tripped-out freaks. Three years ago, we were hobos singing our hearts out about the virtues of the open road. Last year, we were Indians. Now, we're revolutionaries. Man, if the revolution ever comes for real, they'll probably use Andy Warhol munitions. You throw it and this big sign comes on—Pow!"

He sank back into the sofa. His wife and their new baby were back in California, and they left him with the puffy look of someone rendered incomplete. But his apathy was more than the product of separation. The vibes are gone. You don't notice it on their new album right away, but live, that sharp hilarity has given way to something almost laconic. Melodies are shattered, lyrics barely coherent. Oh, the language is stronger (the old Fish cheer now reads, "Gimme an F . . . U . . . etc.," and "that bastard, LBJ" has become "that muthuhfucker"), but the sound is disjointed, dazed. Joe stands limply through most of the set, the swing gone from his body, the muscle in his head rarely flexed.

I asked Joe why his music had changed. He straightened up slowly and took off his hat. "See, we're not what we thought we were."

"How so?"

"Well, two years ago, we believed in music like a God. If you're gonna get into a heavy acid trip, you're gonna get religious. If you stop taking acid, you stop being religious."

"Our audience knew we got stoned and they got stoned and it all worked in a big circle," Barry added.

"Yeah, but music's nothing to believe in. I mean . . . it's just sound."

"Do you feel like quitting now?"

"No, I still dig playing. If it got really bad, I couldn't even get up on stage. But today, the only emotion I associate with music is pleasure. There used to be all kinds of . . . well . . . connotations."

In the distance, we heard a shout that sounded like "Dump the Hump," so we ran to the window and raised the blinds. It was a small march to Times Square, complete with Vietcong flags and a police escort. From the hotel, we could see only a sliver of it. Joe smiled, drew the blinds, and turned the volume of the TV up.

"This is C. J. Fish," Barry was grumbling into the phone. "We didn't get any coffee with that food."

"It's hard to sing for real anymore," Joe said, sinking back onto the couch. "Our music is all noise . . . protest noise."

The bell rang and an old acquaintance offered greetings and news from the barricades. Heavy guerrilla scenes in the East Village; Columbia was perking and almost ready to pour. By the way, could the group make a benefit?

Joe said no, they'd be back in California with their families, and the kid wondered why the Fish weren't doing so many street gigs anymore. Barry explained that rock doesn't work in a charged street situation, because the equipment is expensive and immobile. If the cops come, you can't split with an amp on your back.

The talk returned to politics. "The revolution is just another word for working within the community," the friend incanted.

"Yeah, but I'm not into that anymore," Joe said.

"What are you into?"

"Robin and the kid . . . and me."

"But Joe, other kids are in the streets, and they're gonna be laying down a whole new thing."

"I don't believe in the revolution."

"Hell, you are the revolution. So how can you not believe in it?"

"Because there is no revolution. I'm just living out my life-style. That's what you should be doing."

"Obviously we're using the word differently."

"Look, you want to be a revolutionary? You know what that means? It means time—10, 15 years . . . go back to school. Become a revolutionary in school."

"Why don't you go back to school?"

"Because I've got a career, as a poet, an entertainer, and a musician."

"Yeah, well maybe my career is listening to you. And maybe I have to fight to do that."

"Bullshit. You're no revolutionary. You're just a young American citizen in the twentieth century."

147

The hostility is getting a bit thick, so Barry suggests they split for the photographer's studio. Everyone stands and Joe shoves the hat down over his eyes. "I've been a poet, a guru, a politico," he says. "I'll be anything you want. Tell me what you want me to be."

Nobody answers. "Well, I'm in the entertainment business right now. It just so happens that the people I entertain are freaky."

—1968

CHAPTER 26

Love and Money and the Shoot-out in Marin

SAN RAFAEL, California—This is what it means to be well-off in California. It has nothing to do with driving the right car or living in the right kind of house or receiving the right invitations and answering them the right way. Being well off in California means sun and space, a tender ideology, and plenty of padding so the crowded people and the criminals—especially the criminals—can't possibly intrude.

This metaphor of class and space seems most apparent to me whenever I come west from New York, where crowding is endemic and the same fumes strangle all. In Marin, the hills roll and tumble, and the sun shines in calculated brightness. Marin is full of good places to get stoned in; easy to feel transformed amid all that sequestered ease. And though these places are accessible by freeway—even by bus—you seldom see a man who isn't living well on the street. The niggers of Marin are country hippies. They stay, for the most part, in their own wooded enclaves, and they too are busy being well-off.

I've often wondered why crowded people don't come pouring down from the slopes of San Francisco, and out of the baked Chicano flats. Why not a general invasion of the green zone—even for a day? But it seems to be part of the deal that crowded people stay put. The country protects itself from the city, and soon the city becomes an idea, like ecology, to be studied and directed and reformed by remote control. Crowded people are acknowledged with bumper stickers and benefits, and it's sympathy for the devil as long as they keep their distance. But whenever a crowded person passes through, it

149

makes a little niche. Sometimes it makes a hole, an explosive hole in the green shield. Some of the padding gets ripped away, and then the cops come in. You can tell how serious the rip is by how long it takes the locals to settle down to being mellow again.

Last August 7, a young man with tawny skin walked into the Marin County Civic Center with three guns inside his coat. He walked into court. He said, "This is it." He gave the guns away. Three crowded men held them over five country people: the judge, the assistant district attorney, and three female jurors. They walked into the sunlight. They climbed inside a yellow van. They started the motor up. There was some confusion. The judge died in his robes. The young man died in his tawny skin. Two convicts died in their courtroom fatigues. The jurors lived. The young D.A. lived, his spine severed. The third con, shot bad in the stomach, lived to be accused.

And that evening, the people of Marin took to their happy trails to find that someone had ripped a huge and bloody hole in the shield.

● ● ●

The Civic Center of Marin must be the most mellow courthouse in the world. There is no rhetoric in its function or design. It sits nestled in the sunny side of a hill a few green miles from San Rafael, a concrete cylinder in pink and blue and gold. To reach its gates you pass through landscaped gardens and clusters of trees in bloom. A smell of sweet manure hangs over the lawn, a smell of tended earth. Inside, there are subtropical gardens under plastic arches open to the sky, and the floors are earthen red, and the bathrooms smell faintly of evergreen.

"Beauty is the moving cause of nearly every issue worth the civilization we have," Frank Lloyd Wright told the people of Marin back in 1957, when he first presented his plans for their new Civic Center. Seldom has one man's sense of beauty been more insidiously applied. In the Hall of Justice, form absolves function; everything possible has been done to detoxify the business of dispensing punishment. Bureaus and offices sit off the main arcade like booths at a bazaar. There is a lending library on the top floor and a cafeteria on the third; hidden springs and fountains along the terraces; an exhibit of paintings by local artists on the walls. Even those who have the most to fear from this building have contributed (though not by choice) to its success. Every piece of walnut furniture in every court and office has been carved and polished by an inmate at the California pens.

Jacques Ellul tells us one difference between fascism and the technological state is that fascism is visible. If this is so, Wright must be counted among the architects of the current tyranny, in which dominance is intangible, even to those who rule. His Civic Center is a graceful cabana of slopes and arches. Every detail, from doorknobs to ceiling fixtures, is a fully realized curve. Every structural chord has been resolved. There are no flags or emblems within the building, no quotes from Jefferson in raised letters over the door. These symbols of a punitive past have given way to a lushness so profound that it seems impossible to equate the power in its purpose with the beauty in its line. You walk down its corridors filled with a sense of fluid harmony. I am gentle, smiling, curving like these walls, pink and earthy and at ease.

Of course, the jail is a mite less lush. But even here, all that is possible has been done to spare the rod from those who live outside. Like the rest of the Civic Center, it is functionally invisible. There are no bars because no cell contains a window; only nubby concrete walls, painted tan. The rooftop exercise yard (four walls with wire strung across the top) is invisible from the ground. The prison has its own lobby, its own elevators, and its own video surveillance system. Each prisoner may be observed on closed circuit television. Each courtroom has access to a corridor that leads directly to the cell block, so that suspects may be transferred in complete isolation.

In Marin, each prisoner lives in isolated neutrality. He is denied the privilege of impact, either as an individual or as a class. No one can see him or hear him or feel him unless the state consents. Or unless the prisoner breaks the shield.

● ● ●

Dig it:

Cat bops into court carrying three guns. One sawed-off, all right on! "This is it," he says. Judge and jurors, jive D.A., marched under the eyes of reporters, tourists, and pigs. Through the parking lot. Into the yellow van. BAM. BAMBAM.

Dig it:

HOSTAGE
TELLS TALE
OF TERROR
Judge Calm
Before Death

"Christmas put his left arm around me and in his right hand he had a gun pointed at me and two flares, but he said they were dynamite.

"I believed everything he said and he had the gun pointed at my head and he kind of ducked behind me as we left the courtroom.

"In the truck, the judge, he was sitting in the right rear corner, he said he was sorry us jurors had to go through what we had to go through. And I was thinking, not out loud but to myself, well, if you're going to torture me, just shoot me now. I don't want to be tortured.

"Seconds later, the shotgun blast killed Judge Haley.

"And you know what? When I got home, there was a tooth in my hair and some glass in the tooth.

"This was my first experience on a jury, and believe me, my last."

—from the *San Francisco Examiner*, August 16, 1970

● ● ●

Things have changed since the shoot-out. The Marin County Civic Center now looks like a luxury liner doubling as a battleship. Guards and bailiffs are armed; one judge admits to carrying a gun under his robes. A row of bars has been constructed along the corridor that runs beside the courtrooms. Employees and visitors are pat-searched and passed through a metal detector at the gates. Townspeople can no longer return their library books in the slot outside the Hall of Justice. And reporters who wish to cover trials within the building must be accredited by the county, a process that involves being photographed and fingerprinted.

There has been talk among the more intemperate of keeping trials involving convicted felons behind prison walls. "It is time to rise up, people of Marin," writes Mrs. D. C. Ely, in the *Independent-Journal* of San Rafael. "Why can't we have a small but attractive court area or room inside the walls of all our penal institutions for felons who have stabbed or abused other unfortunates inside the walls of said institutions? The courtroom could be well aired, sunny, and even a few potted plants may help the morale of all present."

Since the shooting and the bombing that demolished a courtroom last October, every visitor to the Civic Center has had some inkling of what it means to live under guard. The people who work inside the building seem bewildered by it all. Of course there is security in a metal detector and an armed guard, but the fact remains: if you need to be protected, you need to feel afraid.

The district attorney, Bruce Bales, seems uneasy at his desk, surrounded by golf and tennis trophies, a stunning view of the Pacific to his right. He is a small man with a face like an earnest Airedale, easy to like and even to believe. Normally, Bales himself would be the prosecuting attorney in the trial of Angela Davis and Ruchell Magee, who are charged with conspiring to kidnap and murder Judge Haley. But last December, he withdrew from the case and the state appointed Albert W. Harris, Jr., an assistant attorney general, in his place. Bales was a close friend of the murdered judge—Haley had been his first employer—and remains close to Gary Thomas, his assistant, who was paralyzed during the break.

"Judge Haley was a real gentleman. That's the irony of it. Of all the judges in the county, he was the most courteous. Conscientious in the extreme. He would extend civil rights to everyone, despite rebukes and . . . oh, things you would never expect to hear inside a courtroom. He was certainly not a tough judge in the sense of piling on punishments. You'd never hear him swear or anything like that. He was a gentleman. Some judges, hell, you can tell if they're former prosecutors, 'cause they're tougher than any cop. Or a legal defender if they're overly lenient. But sitting on the bench, you couldn't tell what his background was. He was a gentleman. But I'm biased. I really liked the guy."

The county would breathe easy with a change of venue, though it cannot legally request one. Removing the trial from Marin would save every taxpayer about $20, but it would also give the county time to regain its battered equilibrium, to get back to being mellow again. Bales, too, could use a cooling out. Even now that he has removed himself from the case, reporters monitor his opinions and every black militant knows him as the man who went to New York to bring Angela Davis back.

"I could have tried it," Bales muses, looking out into his view. "I don't know. I'm glad I got out. For many reasons. For a long time, I still thought I was gonna do it. I couldn't have done it impartially, but . . . I don't know."

"Did the shooting change your head around?"

He looks me in the eye for the first and only time.

"Nope."

● ● ●

"We are not alone. We have allies everywhere. We find our comrades wherever in the world we hear the oppressor's whip. People all over the world are rising up; the tide of revolution is about to sweep the shores of America. A picture is worth a thousand words but action is supreme."

—Huey P. Newton, from his eulogy at the funeral of Jonathan Jackson and William A. Christmas, August 12, 1970

"What of the convicts who died in their attempt to escape, and what of the teenage boy, also killed, who smuggled the guns which made the whole tragic episode possible?

"Surely the Lord God himself challenges us all to say, as Christ did on the cross: 'Father, forgive them for they know not what they do.' "

—from an editorial in the *Independent-Journal*, San Rafael, August 12, 1970

● ● ●

First I show my press card to a guard who checks me off on his list. Then I empty my pockets into a plastic container. Then remove my watch, my ring, my shoes, my belt, and anything else likely to show up on a metal-detector. Once through the machine, I stand in the middle of the corridor with my arms and legs spread apart, while a deputy pats my shoulders and pockets and crotch, with a deferential touch not unlike a handshake. I flash on being a felon, held naked against the wall. The fantasy is exciting (you think I'd bring guns in there?) until I realize that I *am* suspect. The guard searches my hair for weapons. A photographer snaps my picture as I fumble with my belongings, trying to detach my ring from my pen without dropping my shoes. Finally I stagger into court, dragging my belt along the carpet.

The courtroom, like the rest of the building, is sinister in its informality. The judge sits behind a simple wooden desk; you don't rise when he walks into the room. The defendants, their lawyers, and the prosecutor's staff are arranged around a semicircular table that runs the length of the room. The jurors (when there is a jury) sit in nine bucket seats, a short rise above the defense. There is no docket, no banister between the jury and the accused, only a low partition between spectators and officers of the court.

This room seems well equipped to handle a seminar or a minor convocation, but surely not a murder trial. Think of the courts in New York. Think of the room where the hearing to extradite Angela Davis took place: high ceiling, Flash Gordon chandeliers, the Honorable Thomas Dickens presiding in his robes, like the driver of some decaying hansom cab. What has happened to our sense of justice as a vengeful father? It has evolved into this verdant baggie, in which the law can be perceived only as an organic process, a hyacinth. In the California tradition of being-there-first, this is truly the courtroom of the future, with a decor so neutral and a procedure so informal that it's hard to think of death as anything more than an inconvenience, meted out by consensus as the only reasonable alternative to life outside.

I strike up a conversation with a young free-lance reporter. We talk about schizophrenia as a vanguard experience. But our reverie is interrupted by the appearance of two armed deputies, one holding a three-foot length of chain, similar to the one I use when walking my dog. The chain is the first sign that a black man convicted of kidnapping and robbery and attempted rape is about to enter the room. He walks in, already chained at the waist—a thick, flat man with shoulders like a stump. He shoots a smile and a half-raised fist at the audience, and sits in a chair that has been bolted to the floor. The guards wind the chain around his waist, and fluff his shirt over the chain so that it is invisible to the court. All you see if you look at Ruchell Magee is a man sitting calmly in his bucket seat, hands resting on his lap, his shoulders slightly hunched. That, you might assume, would be the natural posture of a man who has spent his lion-years as a con.

Then Angela Davis walks in, unencumbered, and takes a seat at the other end of the room. A smile and a raised clenched fist. Scattered applause. Reporters start to snip. "I heard she had some work done on those teeth of hers." And "I wonder where she found the time to go shopping for that dress." Earl Caldwell, the young black reporter from the *New York Times*, smiles into his lapels.

The judge walks in—a slender, clear-faced man with shoulders like a steam iron. He smiles. He introduces himself. "I'm Judge Alan Lindsay from Alameda County, over here on assignment." He introduces the prosecutor. He smiles again. He speaks softly, almost in a whisper, deferential as the guard who searched me on the way in. Think of him as the perfect dinner guest: attentive, respectable, and more than willing to remain invisible beyond the etiquette of the occasion.

He addresses Ruchell Magee, who is attempting to file another writ demanding the removal of his case into federal court. This document, like all the others Magee has filed in the eight years since his last conviction, is written in a stiff hand on prison stationery, and contains the basis of what Magee regards as his defense: that he is being railroaded by court-appointed lawyers and the "flagrant racism" of the system itself; that the state is attempting to suppress evidence he intends to use in his own behalf; that an attorney, offered him immunity if he would testify that Angela Davis provided him with the gun he held during the escape; that he was threatened with the death penalty when he refused to cooperate; that he is being "criminally oppressed, harassed, and tormented in prison."

The right to conduct your own defense is, in fact, a privilege that may be granted at the court's discretion. Magee's motions, with their blunt, alien style, have not disposed the bench to grant his request. And though it was a writ by Magee that persuaded another judge to remove himself from the case, the prosecuting attorney has said: "The defendant's below average intelligence, subnormal education, inexperience, and indisposition toward courts of law do not adequately equip him to save his life."

Judge Lindsay smiles. He accepts Magee's motion, although the defendant cannot move his arms away from his lap to present it. "We're having some difficulty with the chains," says a court-appointed lawyer for Magee.

"I understand," the judge replies. "Would you furnish Mr. Magee with all necessary assistance?"

I remember the time I spent in Judge Julius Hoffman's court during the Chicago Seven trial. I remember Hoffman's craning presence on the bench. I remember his syntax, the way he chewed attorneys' names like tough meat. Alan Lindsay is as good-tempered as Hoffman was spiteful. Yet, if anything is apparent from the way he runs his court, it is how little it matters what tone the judge maintains. The effect of courtesy is nil: as in Chicago, a man is chained to his seat and denied the right to choose his own representation. As in Chicago, circumstantial evidence is applied to a political intent. Anyone who doubts that this is a political trial should consider the indictment against Angela Davis, which mentions, as "overt acts" to be regarded as evidence of criminal intent, specific speeches and activities on behalf of the Soledad Brothers. The defense should have little trouble establishing—if it is permitted to—that Angela Davis was regarded as a criminal before Jon Jackson ever handled any guns.

She sits at the hemispheric table, looking as she always does in court: alert, assured, and provocative. The judge takes note of her behind his smile, and the guards take note behind their guns, and the reporters take note behind their notes. Sex and race hang in the soft air, contradicting the structural intent of the room and turning the gentle meeting hall, with its placid judge, irrevocably into a court of law.

●   ●   ●

As its major business, the defense files a 27-page statement accusing Judge Lindsay of "biases and prejudices . . . that impede his ability to conduct a fair trial." As evidence, the defense cites his prior association with enforcement agencies, his term as an assistant district attorney in Alameda County, his presence on the Oakland school board during the NAACP's intensive campaign against that city's districting policies, and his presumed loyalty to Ronald Reagan, who appointed Judge Lindsay to the Superior Court in 1967. The defense concludes: "The racism

157

inherent in the American judicial political system is clearly manifested in Judge Lindsay's career, a classic of our time."

It would be 10 days before Judge Lindsay responded to the charges by denying he was prejudiced and insisting he had done nothing in his career to further segregation or racism. It would be another two weeks until a hearing before another judge could be convened. At that hearing, the charge of bias was rejected. Still to be argued are pretrial motions for dismissal of the indictment, for bail, and for the right of Angela Davis to act as co-counsel in her own defense. She, at least, cannot be accused of having a low IQ.

It is unlikely that Judge Lindsay will react with much enthusiasm to the prospect of a series of hearings that could last longer than some trials, but neither is he likely to rush things unceremoniously. Not this judge, who has said, in the tradition of the green shield: "Everybody involved in this matter must not only receive a fair trial, but they must also have the feeling that the trial has been fair."

Today, the only day Judge Lindsay has actually encountered Angela Davis and Ruchell Magee, he adjourns the morning session after 12 minutes. In the afternoon, he returns to announce that he will take the Davis challenge under consideration. He assures Magee that his handwritten motion will also receive its due. He smiles. Then he turns to face the press.

"Indicating we are going to adjourn in a few minutes," he purrs, "everyone will remain with the exception of those necessary to escort Miss Davis and Mr. Magee from the courtroom." Guards assume their places, first undoing Magee and then accompanying Davis out the door. The judge departs, and so do the rest of us—reporters and spectators, artists with sketches of Angela (and none of Magee), ministers and defense committee types, a couple in overalls.

I take the elevator up to the cafeteria for a cup of coffee and fruit salad. I sit looking out on the terrace, with its fountains and gardens. I watch a young mother hold her baby up near the edge of the terrace, looking out over the hilltops into the still-green Pacific and the still-blue sky. She's wearing a poncho and print bells. Her cheeks are the color of the walls around me. I fancy she is happy, with space enough to move and time to be. I fancy she is free.

• • •

Listen, lady:

"Flowers, guitar music, and a priest speaking words of joy contrasted today with the quiet of the mourners at the funeral of Judge Harold J. Haley.

"Reverend John P. Tierney, pastor of St. Sylvester's Catholic Church, urged hundreds of persons who had jammed inside for a funeral mass to rejoice with Judge Haley on his entrance into eternal life.

"The bells in the tower of the First Presbyterian Church across the street from Keaton's Mortuary in San Rafael tolled as the hearse pulled slowly away—preceded down Fifth Avenue by a line of 25 police cars, their flashing red lights emphasizing the silence of their sirens.

"A policeman armed with a rifle stood watch atop San Rafael's City Hall, which was closed to traffic until the funeral procession had passed.

"Judge Haley's parish church in Peacock Gap was already crowded as the hearse and line of cars made their way out of San Pedro Road, through the hills, and along the bay the Judge has known all his life."

—from the *Independent-Journal*, August 10, 1971

CHAPTER 27

That Good Night

NEW MILFORD, Connecticut—Sunday. A clean young man stands in a white gazebo on the town green, facing 400 youngsters and their moms and dads. The young man is Larry Reimer, associate minister of the New Milford Congregational Church. At his behest, the concerned people of Litchfield County in Connecticut have assembled to walk 10 miles around the periphery of town, single file when approaching intersections, for the soul purpose of collecting money to feed the hungry of the world.

"We walk because They walk," says the dispatch in the *New Milford Times*. "They—the hungry—walk everywhere they go: many miles to get wood or water; to the fields they cultivate; as they hoe or plow; to get medical aid if it is available (at times as far as 50 miles); to school, if they have one. But just walking isn't going to feed hungry children. What will feed them is food, purchased by getting sponsors to pledge."

Here is how the money is raised: each walker procures a sponsor who pledges between $1 and $10 for every mile traversed. Generally, the route comprises 10 miles, but the walkers can cover twice that distance if the weather is good and the pop is plentiful and the occasion carries with it enough goodwill. In the past year, there have been 134 such excursions throughout America, and more than 35,000 people—mostly young people but occasionally whole families and even the elderly—are walking together for hunger.

"You know that half the world is hungry," the pledge cards read: "That entire nations exist on a starvation diet . . . that 17 million refugees have no home or security . . . that at least 10,000 people starve to death daily . . . that at least five persons died while you read this. Be an agent of change!" No one in New Milford seems to know how the money that is being collected this afternoon will reach the wretched of the earth, although an account has been opened at the Colonial Bank. It is a little like the March of Dimes: folks make a contribution with a general understanding that good works will ensue. Everyone has seen hunger on television, and everyone wants to do something about it, and now there is an organization called CROP, which is the Community Hunger Appeal of the Church World Service, an arm of the National Council of Churches of Christ. CROP is coordinating today's walk, along with the ministers of the New Fairfield Congregational, Kent Congregational, Gaylordsville Methodist, New Milford Congregational, and Roman Catholic ("I think it's St. Michael's," says one minister) churches. In addition, the township of Kent has donated one school bus, and the town of New Milford has contributed one engine of the Water Witch Hose Company. "They don't believe in separation of church and state around here," says a man in walking shorts distributing leaflets on the green. He may be a minister.

"I really wanna thank all of you for turning out. This is an exciting thing," says Larry Reimer, who recruited nearly 100 student volunteers at a compulsory high school assembly. "Larry is very mod," says Reverend Cal Ukena of the Sherman Congregational Church, the only minister present this afternoon who is actually wearing a clerical collar. Larry Reimer is wearing an old pair of jeans with pocket patches in railroad stripes, an Oxford blue button-down shirt, and old hiking boots. He is 27 years old. He wears his blond hair in a long pageboy.

"I don't know if we could have done a peace thing this year," he confides. "I thing we're out of confrontation politics now, and we're into a more personal thing. There's more of a turn inward. People are getting their heads together, doing a lot of nonverbal stuff."

Two years ago, Larry Reimer arrived in New Milford from the Yale Divinity School. That was the year of the Great Moratorium, and Larry helped organize a candlelight vigil in the green, and his youth group collected 600 signatures against the war. Two years ago, folks were talking about ad hoc politics and civil disobedience, and when the campuses erupted over Cambodia and Kent, people opened up their pockets and their hearts.

Larry concedes he misses all that now, but he is willing to settle for a lesser intensity of good works, in keeping with the chastened enthusiasm of the time. "People want to do something more concrete now, like collecting $50 for the hungry," he explains. Larry's Social Action Committee is no longer gathering signatures against the war; this year it is sponsoring housing for the elderly. Larry's congregation is no longer lighting candles in the green; instead, it is holding experimental worship services every fourth Sunday, taking trust walks, and performing exercises from *What to Do Until the Messiah Comes*. The Sunday school has abolished grading and substituted a voluntary attendance program. This month's unit is "God's Garden: Our World," in which young people take pollution walks and build a "garbage garden" of items littering their town.

"It's all consciousness raising. Some people get it through the ecology issue. Some people get it through women's lib. You know, I meet a lot of women saying, what am I doing with my life, so I've started a consumer group investigating pricing at supermarkets. It builds a sense of identity to get involved.

"It's not as radical a thing, but I think it's all right."

On the green a line of perhaps 350 walkers has formed. Each person carries a placard identifying a sponsor, so that the march looks vaguely political until you get up close. There is a faint restlessness to get the afternoon under way. An old man is walking with his gray poodle. A black man in a cowboy hat is carrying a leather golf stool in his hand. Only 20 or 30 people remain sitting on the green, and these are mostly freaks who have come to mingle and deal. Even though freaks carry drugs, most folks in New Milford regard them with compassion, as wanderers looking for the promise of belonging. There have been some arrests.

Police Chief James Mancusi, who played Tevye earlier this year in a town production of *Fiddler on the Roof*, climbs into his car at the head of the march and leads the way. The line will proceed down Lower Grove Street, to Landsville Road, through Harry Brook Park, back along Lanesville past Lover's Leap (where legend has it that two Indian lovers from warring tribes . . .) down Lover's Leap Road, along Town Farm Road, and then back to the green via Highway 67. The march will take about three hours. At four points along the route, the town has set up validation points offering refreshments, and there are two first aid vans accompanying the line.

It's a pretty day, cool and willowy. People are swinging their arms, sipping pop, skipping in step. Barechested guys with jeans pulled down below their navels. Girls throwing caution and Dentine to the winds. No one is smoking. There are T-shirts inscribed "Vote." A random 10-speed. Cameras and transistors. Flushed cheeks and modest perspiration. Sneakers with stars and stripes.

Back on the green, the crowd regroups for Kool-aid and compassion. "Let's give ourselves a hand," Larry Reimer says, and there is some applause. A band called Pilot is offering its services free. Chief Mancusi points his finger at a freak and smiles. The afternoon is mellowing into dusk. No one knows yet how much money has been raised, but everyone seems pleased with the results. For a while, there is no noise aside from the music, and everyone is sitting close and tired in the grass, and there is a faint aroma of campfire, and a moment passes, brief and hard to capture, of sheer, still comfort. Belonging. Success.

United we stand
Divided we fall
C'mon people
Let's get on the ball
Let's get together
Yeah, c'mon let's get together
Because together we will stand
Every boy girl woman or man.

—1970

A Note on the Text

Since the founders of the *Village Voice* did not believe in editing, many of these pieces were originally published exactly as they came out of my typewriter. I've chosen to compensate retrospectively for that, by trimming extraneous phrases, sentences, and the occasional paragraph or two. In addition, I've omitted arcane references and expressions (who was Eve Democracy?) and, in a few cases, changed them into something approaching contemporary slang. My intention is to sharpen the descriptions in these pieces and to strengthen the narrative. As if remastering a collection of golden oldies, I've muted the strings to bring up the vocals. But the song remains the same.

INDEX

acid house, xiv
Albin, Peter, 16, 19
Alice in Wonderland (British TV production), 72
American Bandstand, 15
Animals, The, 63
Anthpacak, Jan, 64
Antoine, ix, 67–70
Aristotle, 34
Armed Forces Radio, 59
Arthur Becker Clubhouse, 60
Asia House, 71
assassinations, xx

Bales, Bruce, 153–4
Balin, Marty, 56
"Ball and Chain" (Big Brother and the Holding Company), 18
"Ballad of the Green Berets" (Barry Sadler), 67
Balloon Farm, 89–93
bands
    Animals, 63
    The Band, 143
    Beach Boys, 57, 85, 88
    The Beatles, xviii, 13, 36, 56, 85, 86, 143
    Big Brother and the Holding Company, 15–19, 57
    Blues Project, 50
    The Byrds, 56, 57, 70, 84, 143
    The Charlatans, 53
    Country Joe and the Fish, 56, 145–8
    Cream, 144
    The Doors, 36–40, 144
    The Fugs, 70
    The Grateful Dead, 55, 56, 58, 86
    Jefferson Airplane, 53, 55, 57
    Die Kandles, 60
    The Kinks, 63, 64
    Lovin' Spoonful, 65

Luke and the Apostels, 102
The Mandalas, 102
Martha and the Vandellas, 77
Mefisto, 64
The Monkees, xiv, 54
The Olympiks, 62–5
Paul Butterfield Blues Band, 56
Paul Revere and the Raiders, 77
The Paupers, 102
The Primitives, 91
Quicksilver Messenger Service, 57
The Rascals, 50
The Rolling Stones, 3, 6, 9–14, 36, 56, 60
Sonny and Cher, 43, 92
Sopwith Camel, 53, 57
The Sputniks, 63
The Velvet Underground, 50, 90–3
The Yardbirds, 75
Band, The, 143
Barney's Beanery, 109
Barry, Len, 46
Beach Boys, 57, 85, 88
Beatles, The, xviii, 13, 36, 56, 85, 86, 143
Beck, Jeff, 75
Berry, Chuck, 77
Big Brother and the Holding Company, 15–19, 57
bikers
    Hells Angels, 99
    Vagabonds (Toronto), 107
"The Birth of the Haight" (happening), 99
Black Panthers, 125, 138
blacks
    and Columbia University, 132–3
    and hippies, 121
    Chicago Southern Christian Leadership Conference march, 125–9
    sixties experience, xiv

167

Blues Project, 50
Brown, H. Rap, 132–3
Burr, Henry, 26
Burroughs, William, 50
Byrds, The, 56, 57, 70, 84, 143

Cabinet of Dr. Caligari (film), 81
Caldwell, Earl, 156
Cale, John, 91–3
Calloway, Cab, 25
Cambodia, 163
Canada, 101–8
Carmichael, Stokley, 133
Carson, Johnny, 21, 22, 30, 88
Cassen and Stern (light shows), 83–4
Cassen, Jackie, 83–4
Celebration of the Lizard, The (Jim
    Morrison), 33
Chapman, Brian (Blues), 105–7
Charlatans, The, 53
Cher, 43, 92
Chicago (city), 125–9
    1968 Democratic convention, xx,
        137–41, 145
Christmas, William A., 152, 154
civil rights, xix, 125–9
Clark, Dick, 76
Clarke, Alan, 105
clothing, counterculture, 3–7
    hip huggers, 5
    tie-dye, xiii
Coey, Walter, 120
Columbia Records, 41–6, 54
Columbia University, 131–6, 137, 140
Columbo, Russ, 25
Communication Company, 96
community action, 161–4
Company of Young Canadians,
    105–7
cooperatives, 98
Copland, Aaron, 92
Country Joe and the Fish, 56, 145–8
Cream, 144
Crop (Community Hunger Appeal
    of the Church World Service),
    162
Crowther, Bosley, 81
Czechoslavakia, 61–5

dances
    The Gobble, 89
    The Twist, 64
Davidoff, Sid, 135

Davis, Angela, xx, 153–8
Davis, Sammy, Jr., 47
De Blasio, Ron, 25, 26, 28, 30
De Poe, Dave, 105–7
Death of the Mind (mixed-media
    presentation), 83
Democratic convention
    1960, xvii
    1968 (Chicago), xx, 137–41
De Nave, Connie, 75
Denmark, 67
Densmore, John, 36, 39
Dickens, Thomas, 155
Didion, Joan, xvi
Diggers
    San Francisco, 95–100
    Toronto, 103–8
Dion, xvii
Dom, 89–93
Doors, The, 36–40, 144
Doster, Betsy, 10
Dover, Derry (*see* Tiny Tim)
draft dodgers, 102
Dreja, Chris, 75
drugs
    and the Maharishi Mahesh Yogi, 87
    and music, 55–6
    Ecstasy, xiv
    LSD, 81
    methedrine, 122
    psychedelic, 55; as marketing
        device, 81–4
Duncan, Gary, 57
Dylan, Bob, 30, 50, 56, 68, 76, 89, 91

Earth Rose (Venice, Calif., head
    shop), 111
East Berlin, 59–61
Ecstasy, xiv
Edison's Electric Machine, 15, 16
Edouard, 68
Electric Factory, 15
Elektra Records, 54
Ellus, Jacques, 151
Les Elucubrations d'Antoine (Antoine),
    67
Esquire. xv, xvii
"Exploding Plastic Inevitable"
    (happening), 92

Family Dog Productions, 16–17, 95
Fantastic Voyage (film), 81
Fitzpatrick, Linda, 119–20

'49ers (Canadian hippies), 102, 107
France, 67–8
Freaks (Los Angeles hippies), 113–17
Free Frame of Reference, 97
Friendship Missionary Baptist
     Church, 126
Fugs, The, 70

Galahad (New York hippie), 120,
     121, 122
Garcia, Jerry, 56
Geldzahler, Henry, 90
Germany
   East, 59–61
   West, 67
Getz, Dave, 18
Gilgour, Robert, 102, 104
Ginsberg, Allen, 50, 65
Girl on F Street (film), 114
"Give Me More of Your Love" (The
     Sputniks, 63
Gleason, Ralph, 54, 57, 98
Goldstein, Richard, ix–x, xii–xxi
Gottehrer, Barry, 135
Graham, Bill, 55
Graham, Billy, 87
Grateful Dead, The, 55, 56, 58, 86
Grogan, Emmett, 95–7

Haight Ashbury, 95–100
Haley, Judge Harold J., 152–9
Halliday, Johnny, 67, 68
Hamill, Pete, 48
"Hanky Panky" (Tommy James and
     the Shondells), 60
happenings, 69, 92, 99
"Hard Rain's Gonna Fall" (Bob
     Dylan), 68
Hardin, Tim, 50, 51–2
Harper's, xv
Harper's Bazaar, 19
Harris, Albert W., Jr., 153
Harrison, George, 71, 73
"Hello, Hello" (Sopwith Camel), 57
Hells Angels, 99, 138
Helms, Chet, 16–17, 95
"Help" (The Beatles, The Olympiks),
     64
Hendrix, Jimi, 132
"Hey, Jude" (The Beatles), 143
Hit Parader (magazine), 11
HIP (Haight Independent
     Proprieters), 95

hippies, 95–100, 101–8, 138
Hoffman, Abbie, 121
Hoffman, Judge Julius, 157
"Horse Latitudes" (The Doors), 37–8
Howard Presbyterian Church, 95,
     100
Hullabaloo, 89
Hutchinson, James Leroy
     ("Groovy"), 119–22

I Protest!, xx

Jackson, George, xx
Jackson, Jonathan, 154, 157
Jagger, Mick, 6, 9, 10, 11, 13
Jameson, Frederic, xviii
Janda, Petr, 62, 63, 65
Janis Gallery, 69
Jefferson Airplane Takes Off, 55
Jefferson Airplane, The, 53, 55, 57
The Joe Pyne Show, 114
Johnson, Betty, 69
Johnson, Lyndon, 88, 110
Jones, Anita, 26
Jones, Brian, 7, 9, 11, 13, 14
Joplin, Janis, 15–19
journalism, xv–xxi, xxi
"Juanita Banana" (The Peels), 67

Kaleidoscope (film), 81
Kama Sutra Records, 53
Die Kandles, 60
Kauffman, Irving, 26
Kaury, Herberto Buckingham (*see*
     Tiny Tim)
Kennedy, John F., xiv, xvii
Kensington Market, 102
Kent State, Ohio, murders at, 163
Kerson, Mary, 103, 108
Kesey, Ken, 56
Khan, Ali Akbar, 72
King, Martin Luther, 125–9, 139
Kinks, The, 63, 64
Kirk, Grayson, 132, 135, 136
Klien, Ladislav, 63–4
Koppel, Ted, xxi
Kramer, John, 41–6
Krieger, Robbie, 36–39

Lamport, Alan, 106
LAPD (Los Angeles Police
     Department), 110–11
Las Vegas, 21

Laurel Canyon, 109, 112
League for Spiritual Discovery, 83
Leary, Timothy, 81–3
Lee, Brenda, 6
Lennon, John, 30
Les Crane Show, 49
Lindsay, Judge Alan, 156–8
Lindsay, x (New York mayor), 119, 135
Los Angeles, 57, 109–12, 113–17
Los Angeles Free Press, 104, 110, 111
Love, Larry (*see* Tiny Tim)
Lovin' Spoonful, 65
LSD–I Hate You (film), 81
Luke and the Apostles, 102

MacDonald, Country Joe (*see also* Country Joe and the Fish), ix, 145–8
Magee, Ruchell, 155–8
Maharishi Mahesh Yogi, 85–8
Mailer, Norman, xvi, xvii
Malanga, Gerard, 90–3
Malcé, Michael, 49
Malcom X, 133
Mancusi, James, 163, 164
Mandalas, The, 102
Mante, Bruce, 120
Manzarek, Ray, 36, 39
Marat/Sade, xiv–xv
Marin County Civic Center, 150–3, 155
Marin County, Calif., 149–59
Married . . . with Children, xiii
Martha and the Vandellas, 77
McCartney, Paul, 6
McLuhan, Marshall, 73, 83, 103
McNeill, Don, xix
Mefisto, 64
Melton, Barry, 145, 148
Metesky, George, 98
"Metesky, Miss," 97–100
"Midnight Hour" (Grateful Dead), 58
Mighty Blackstone Rangers, 126
Millbrook, 83
Moby Grape, 53–4, 56
Mondo Bizarro (film), 114
Monkees, The, xiv, 54
Monterey Pop Festival, 18
Moratorium, The Great, 162
Morrison, Jim, 33–40
Morrison, Sterling, 91–3

"The Moving Finger Writes" (Len Barry), 46
"The Moving Finger Writes" (John Kramer), 43, 44, 45
Murray, the K, 50, 51–2
Murray, Billy, 26
Murrow, Ed, xxi
music
    and violence, 38
    Acid House, xiv
    art rock, 144
    blues, 17
    rock, xix; and record industry, xix; in Eastern bloc countries, 59–65
    promotion, 75–8
    raga sound, 72–4
    rock 'n' roll, xvii
    San Francisco sound, 53–8
music venues
    Anderson (New York), 18
    Arthur Becker Clubhouse (East Berlin), 60
    Avalon Ballroom (San Francisco), 18, 53, 58, 95
    Balloon Farm (Manhattan), 89–93
    Caesar's Palace (Las Vegas), 21, 24, 27
    Cheetah (New York), 84
    Circus Maximus (Las Vegas), 30
    The Dom (Manhattan), 89–93
    Electric Factory (Philadelphia), 15–16, 18
    Felt Forum, 88
    Fillmore (San Francisco), 53, 55, 58
    Page Three (New York), 27
    Peppermint Lounge (Manhattan), 50
    Philharmonic Hall, 72–3
    The Scene (Manhattan), 47, 50
musicians
    Albin, Peter, 16, 19
    Anthpacak, Jan, 64
    Antoine, ix, 67–70
    Balin, Marty, 56
    Barry, Len, 46
    Beck, Jeff, 75
    Berry, Chuck, 77
    Cale, John, 91–3
    Calloway, Cab, 25
    Cher, 43, 92
    Copland, Aaron, 92
    Davis, Sammy, Jr., 47

Densmore, John, 36, 39
Dion, xvii
Dreja, Chris, 75
Dylan, Bob, 30, 50, 56, 68, 76, 89, 91
Edouard, 68
Garcia, Jerry, 56
Getz, Dave, 18
Hardin, Tim, 50, 51–2
Harrison, George, 71, 73
Hendrix, Jimi, 132
Jagger, Mick, 6, 9, 10, 11, 13
Janda, Petr, 62, 63, 65
Jones, Brian, 7, 9, 11, 13, 14
Joplin, Janis, 15–19
Kauffman, Irving, 26
Khan, Ali Akbar, 72
Klien, Ladislav, 63–4
Kramer, John, 41–6
Krieger, Robbie, 36, 39
Lee, Brenda, 6
Lennon, John, 30
MacDonald, Country Joe, ix, 145–8
Manzarek, Ray, 36, 39
McCartney, Paul, 6
Morrison, Jim, 33–40
Morrison, Sterling, 91–3
Murray, Billy, 26
Nico, 68, 91–3
Noone, Peter, 76
Presley, Elvis, 25, 36, 37, 64, 67
Redding, Otis, 17
Reed, Lou, 91–3
Richard, Keith, 75
Sam the Sham, 45
Shankar, Ravi, 71–4
Smith, Bessie, 17
Smith, Kate, 77
Svoboda, Karel, 64
Tiny Tim, 21–31
Valee, Rudy, 26
Waters, Muddy, 50
Watts, Charlie, 9, 11, 12
Weir, Bob, 55, 56
Wilson, Brian, 57
Wyman, Bill, 9, 11
Yanovsky, Zal, 6
"My Best Friend" (Jefferson Airplane), 55

National Guard, 88
New Journalism, x, xv–xvii, xx

New Journalists, xv–xvii
New Milford Community Church, 161
New Milford, Conn., 161–4
New York Post, 51
New York Times, 47
Newsweek, 47, 50, 53
Newton, Huey P., 154
Nico, 68, 91–3
Nietzsche, Friedrich, 34
"Nineteenth Nervous Breakdown" (Rolling Stones), 12
Nixon, Richard, xx
Noone, Peter, 76
O'Brien, Geoffrey, xiii
Oldham, Andrew Loog, 9, 12
Olympiks, 62–5
"One Hundred Men and One Command" (German version of "Ballad of the Green Berets"), 67
The Oracle, 95

Paraphernalia (boutique), 69
Paul Butterfield Blues Band, 56
Paul Revere and the Raiders, 77
Paul, Steve, 47–52
Paulekas, Godo, 113, 115–17
Paulekas, Sue, 114, 116, 117
Paulekas, Vitautus Alphonsus (Vito), 113–17
Paupers, The, 102
Peace and Freedom Party, 112
Perry, Richard, 23, 26
Philadelphia, 15–16
police, 97, 99
    Chicago Democratic convention, 138–9
    Columbia University, 134–5
    Los Angeles, 110–11
    San Francisco, 97, 99
    Toronto, 104–7
politics
    community action, 161–4
    conservative, xv
    eighties *vs.* sixties, xiv
pop
    (concept), xviii
    culture, radicalization of, 143–4
Pop (magazine), 6
"Pop Eye," xix
Port Arthur, Texas, 17
Prague, Czechoslovakia, 61–5
Presley, Elvis, 25, 36, 37, 64, 67

Primitives, The, 91
Prince Philip, 30
Princess Margaret, 30
psychedelic drugs, 55
    as marketing device, 81–4
Psychedelic Celebrations, 82
Psychedelic Shop, 95
Pyne, Joe, 114

Quicksilver Messenger Service, 57

Radio Free Europe, 62
Radio Luxembourg, 62
Radio Prague, 64
"raga sound," 72
Ramparts (magazine), 53
Rascals, The, 50
Rave (magazine), 10
Ray, Satyajit, 72
RCA Records, 53
Reagan, Ronald, 157
record companies
    Columbia Records, 41–6, 54
    Elektra Records, 54
    Kama Sutra Records, 53
    RCA Records, 53
    Sunbeam Music, 41
    Supraphon Records, 64
    Warner Brother Records, 68
record industry, xix, 41–6
Redding, Otis, 17
Reed, Lou, 91–3
Reimer, Larry, 161–4
Relf, Keith, 75
"revolution," ix, 145, 147
"Revolution" (The Beatles), 143
Richard, Keith, 9, 10
riots
    Chicago (1968 Democratic
        convention), 137–41
    Chicago (Gage Park), 127–9 1966
    Columbia University, 131–6
    police, 104–7, 110–11
    Toronto, 104–7
Roberts, Howard, 43
Rolling Stone, xix
Rolling Stones, The, 3, 6, 9–14, 36,
    56, 60
Rothchild, Paul, 38, 39
Rudd, Mark, 144

Saint Mark's Place, 89
Sales, Soupy, 25

Sam the Sham, 45
San Francisco Chronicle, 54
San Francisco Mime Troupe, 54, 96
San Francisco, 16, 95–100
    music underground, 53–8
    North Beach, 54–5
San Rafael, Calif., 149–59
"Satisfaction" (Rolling Stones), 12,
    14, 61
Scene, The, 47–8
Schaap, Dick, 48
SDS (Students for a Democratic
    Society), 132
Shango (African god of thunder), 9
Shankar, Ravi, 71–4
Shrimpton, Chrissie, 6
Simon, Paul, 56
sitar, 71, 74
sixties revival, xiii, xiv
Smith, Bessie, 17
Smith, Kate, 77
Smothers Brothers, xiv
Sonny and Cher, 43, 92
Sontag, Susan, xvi
Sopwith Camel, 53, 57
Sounds from Big Pink (The Band), 143
South Africa, 67
Southern Christian Leadership
    Conference, 125–9
Spiritual Regeneration Movement,
    85
Sputniks, The, 63
Stern, Rudi, 83–4
Stevens, Gary, 12
The Strait Theatre, 98
student protest, 131–6
Sullivan, Ed, 13
Sunbeam Music, 41
"Sunny Afternoon" (The Kinks; The
    Olympiks), 64
Supraphon Records
    (Czechoslovakia), 64
Surrealistic Pillow (Jefferson
    Airplane), 55
Svoboda, Karel, 64
Sweetheart of the Rodeo (The Byrds),
    143

Talese, Gay, xvi, xvii
television news, xvi
television shows
    Alice in Wonderland (British TV), 72
    American Bandstand, 15

172

Hullabaloo, 89
Joe Pyne Show, 114
Johnny Carson Show, 21, 22, 30, 88
Les Crane Show, 49
Man from UNCLE, 4
Married . . . with Children, xiii
Merv Griffin Show, 4, 81
The Monkees, xiv, 54
television, trash, xxi
theater
  Marat/Sade, xiv–xv
Thelin brothers, 95
"These Boots Were Made for
  Walking" (Nancy Sinatra), 67
Thomas, Gary, 153
Thompson, Hunter, x, xvi
Thorburn, David (introduction by),
  ix–x
Tierney, John P., 159
"The Times They Are a-Changin'"
  (Bob Dylan), 68
Tiny Tin (Herberto Buckingham
  Kaury), 21–31
Tompkins Square Park, 119–21
Toronto, 101–8
Trips Festival (San Francisco), 16

UCLA film school, 35, 36
Ukena, Cal, 162
"underground," 53
Unter Den Linden, East Berlin, 59

Vagabonds (Canadian bikers), 102
Vallee, Rudy, 26

Velvet Underground, The, 50, 90–3
Venice, Calif., 111–12
Venice Survival Committee, 112
Vietnam War, xix, 65
Village Bar Association (Toronto),
  103, 107
Village Voice, The, ix, xv, xvii–xix
Vinyl (Andy Warhol film), 90

Wallace, George, 112, 126, 144
Warhol, Andy, 50, 51, 90–1, 93, 146
Warner Brothers, 68
Waters, Muddy, 50
Watts, Charlie, 9, 11, 12
Weir, Bob, 55, 56
"White Rabbit" (Jefferson Airplane),
  55
Whitman, Walt, xvi
Williams, Tennessee, 47, 83
Wilson, Brian, 57
WKCR, 133, 136
WMCA, 81
Wolfe, Tom, x, xvi, xix
Wright, Frank Lloyd, 150
Wyman, Bill, 9, 11

Yanovsky, Zal, 6
Yardbirds, The, 75–8
yippies (Youth International Party),
  xix
Yorkville Avenue (Toronto), 101–8

Zugsmith, Albert, 81